Norse Mythology for Kids

NORSE MYTHOLOGY
FOR KIDS

TALES OF GODS, CREATURES, AND QUESTS

MATHIAS NORDVIG, PHD

ILLUSTRATIONS BY MEEL TAMPHANON

ROCKRIDGE
PRESS

Interior Designer: Jane Archer and Scott Petrower
Cover Design: Jane Archer
Art Producer: Samantha Ulban
Editor: Sean Newcott
Production Editor: Matthew Burnett
Illustrations by © 2020 Meel Tamphanon.
Author photograph courtesy of © Erica Lindberg.

ISBN: Print 978-1-64611-853-3 | eBook 978-1-64611-854-0
R0

This book is dedicated to the
great Danish storyteller
HENNING KURE

CONTENTS

SÆL!

Welcome, fellow Vikings! The word *sæl* means "happy" and was a common greeting among Scandinavians a thousand years ago, during the Viking Age.

Anyone who lived in Scandinavia—the countries now known as Denmark, Norway, Sweden, and Iceland—during the years 800 to 1066 was considered a Viking. The Vikings, also called the Norse, are legendary as raiders, explorers, warriors, and poets, and they believed that the gods they worshipped had these same characteristics. They told stories, or myths, about Thor, Odin, Frigg, and many other fierce and fearless gods and goddesses. In Scandinavia, these stories are still told today. Norse myths are taught in schools and featured in movies, comics, books, and songs.

These myths could have been lost forever, but fortunately, the kings and leaders of Scandinavia in the Viking Age had *skalds*—court poets who told stories and wrote poetry about the ancient Nordic gods and heroes. Even when the Viking Age came to a close and Scandinavians adopted Christianity as their religion, these stories were still important enough to be written down. It's because they were recorded that these incredible myths are still told today.

The myths of the Nordic gods were saved in books like the *Poetic Edda*, which is a collection of poetry from Iceland. Also from Iceland is the *Prose Edda*, which was written by a chieftain, or warlord, named Snorri Sturluson. He lived in the 1200s, and he used the poetry from the Poetic *Edda* and the old *skalds* to write captivating stories about the Nordic gods. Sturluson's parents probably taught him these stories when he was a child, too.

It is no surprise that the many diverse descendants of the Vikings enjoy the stories about the Nordic gods. Norse myths are full of magic, love, sorrow, betrayal, war, heroism, and triumph. They are timeless and exciting, and to a historian like Snorri Sturluson, Thor and Odin and others were not only gods, they were special people who lived in bygone days. Myths speak to the wonder of the world, teach us valuable lessons about life, and inspire us to do great things.

This book retells these classic tales, taking inspiration from the *Poetic Edda* and *Prose Edda*, Scandinavian folktales and sagas, and a portion of imagination—because to Scandinavians, these stories are still alive.

As you begin reading, you will step into the universe of the ancient Viking gods, a world filled with fantastic beings: gods, giants, trolls, ogres, elves, dwarfs, and monsters. There is the fearless Thor who battles dark forces. There is Odin, the wise rune-master. There is Freya, who is known for her great beauty and fierce nature. There is Frigg, the loving mother, and her son Balder, who meets a tragic fate in battle. There is Loki, the chaotic trickster. There is Njord, the lord of ships, and his powerful wife Skadi, the mountain princess. And we will meet many other great gods, goddesses, creatures, and monsters along the way. Let's go now to the enchanting and wild world of Norse mythology.

THE CREATION
OF THE WORLD

obody really knows how the world began. Some say that in the beginning there was only a deep, deep sea called Ginnungagap, and then Jord, the daughter of Sky and the mother of Earth, fell from above and landed in the ocean. She swam around for some time until Loon came flying by. Jord and Loon talked for a while and decided to build Earth because it would be nice for Loon to have a place to stretch her legs when she was not swimming or flying.

Loon dove down into the sea and reached the bottom of the ocean to pick up some mud and bring it back to the surface. Jord put the mud on her body and created Earth: Her flesh became the soil, her teeth the rocks, and her bones the mountains. The blood that flowed in her veins was the water that came from the rivers of the mountains, the lakes, and the marshes. Underneath the ocean floor and deep within Jord, a fire burned. To the north, it was very cold, and ice built up.

After some time passed, Jord gave birth to a Jotun named Ymir. Ymir knew about the fire burning deep within Jord because he came from inside her, and when he traveled the lands, he discovered the ice in the north. Ymir began to create many beings from this fire and ice. The beings he made are called Jotnar. Ymir created Surt and sent him to the caves in the ground, where he ruled over the flames in Muspellheim. Ymir also created Hrimnir and gave him power over the ice. He created so many Jotnar that they became impossible to count, and in the end, the world was full of fire and ice.

Ymir's son, Bolthorn, had a daughter named Bestla, who cared for the cow Audhumbla. This cow lived off stones. On the first day that Audhumbla licked a certain rock, a head came out. On the second day, Audhumbla licked the rock again and the upper body came free, and on the third day Audhumbla licked the rock, the legs were free, too. The man who came from the stone was named Burr. He married Bestla and they had three sons: Odin, Vili, and Ve. We call them the sons of Burr.

Since the ground was frozen everywhere, except for those places where Surt's fire came out, no one except Hrimnir's kin and Surt's kin was happy in that world. The sons of Burr realized that something had to be done, so they decided to kill Ymir, who was the source of all this chaos. When they found Ymir, they stabbed him with their spears. His blood gushed out over the world and became the oceans, drowning many of the Jotnar. Then the sons of Burr took Ymir's skull and made the blue heaven from it, with his brains as the gray clouds. They took molten sparks from Surt's fire and placed them on the inside of Ymir's skull—these became the stars at night.

Finally, the sons of Burr found two elves and gave them two of Surt's greater sparks, so that they could ride across the sky in their chariots and light up the sky. This is how the sons of Burr created night and day.

The sons of Burr decided to call the first part of the day "morning," and the next part "midday." They called the third part "noon" and the fourth part "evening." The last part was called "night." The sons of Burr set the course of the sun and moon and put the god Mundilfari in charge of counting time—that is how they created the years.

Then the sons of Burr gathered on the eternal plains, Idavoll, to build their houses and temples. They created workshops for iron and gold. They walked across the world and sowed plants and trees: spruce, pine, birch, beech, ash, and oak. When the sun shone on the ground, the green plants grew tall and lush. The mightiest of these plants was Yggdrasill, which means "the measuring tree." It stood, evergreen, at the center of the world, with a trunk that shone white as crystal, and all the universe revolved around it. From its leaves fell the morning dew that landed in the lush valleys. At its top, a mighty eagle was perched, and when he flapped his wings, he sent winds across our world. Yggdrasill's roots reached deep into the soil, and below them lay the serpent Nidhogg.

At the foot of the tree, in a place called Urd's Well, the goddesses of fate met. These goddesses were called Norns, and there were three of them: Past, Present, and Future. The Norns decided the fate of humans and wrote their decisions in magical symbols called runes.

The sons of Burr gave dwellings to the dwarfs and the elves in the ground. This underground land was called Nidavellir. Dwarfs and elves were given a shape that resembled humans, but the dwarfs couldn't come out of Nidavellir in the daytime because the sunlight turned them to stone, but the elves could. It is said that if you have second sight—a sort of psychic ability—you can see the dwarfs and be their friend. Dwarfs and elves live all around us in the rocks and the trees and the soil under our feet.

There were so many dwarfs and elves that no one could remember all their names, but some of them were called New-moon, Moon-wane, North and South, East and West, Dawdler, Trembler, Grumbler, Friend, Mead-wolf, Wand-elf, Spurt, Wise, and Bright. There was also Craftsman, Waster, Mud-plain, Swift, Warrior, Oak-shield, Frosty, and Artisan. They could help the gods when needed and that was exactly what they did for the goddess Sif.

Sif had long, golden locks that were so beautiful that the trickster god Loki wanted them for himself. So one day, while Sif slept, Loki cut off all her hair. When Sif woke up and went to the river to bathe, she realized that she no longer had any hair. She was furious! She quickly discovered that it was Loki who had stolen it. By then, Loki had changed shape to become a swallow and built himself a nest out of the hair, so Sif sat by the nest and waited for him. When he came out, she caught him in a basket and brought him to Thor, the god of thunder, for punishment.

Thor stuck his hand in the basket and squeezed so hard around the little bird that he couldn't make a sound. Then Thor took him out of the basket and said, "Loki, I know it is you! You will give Sif her hair back, or I will squeeze you so hard that you die!" Loki agreed to to give Sif her hair back, but he had a trick up his sleeve. He took the form of a snake, crawled into a hole in the ground, and went all the way down to Nidavellir.

In Nidavellir, he found the dwarfs Brokk and Eitri, two crafty brothers. Loki made a bet with them: "I bet that you two can't make a hammer so strong that not even Thor can break it, and I bet that you two can't make a spear so light that Odin can throw it across the world, and I bet that you can't make golden strings more beautiful than Sif's hair." Brokk and Eitri looked at the snake and said, "We bet you that we can make these things. And if we win this bet, we shall have your head as our prize!" Loki agreed to these terms, and they all went to Odin, the ruler of the gods, to swear on it.

The dwarfs were given the time between two full moons to complete their task. First, Eitri put bones in the forge, which was a furnace used to construct things, while Brokk worked the bellows. While they were busy, Loki took the shape of a fly and flew over and sat on Brokk's arm. The fly bit him, but Brokk didn't notice it. Eitri took out his masterpiece—a skillfully made sturdy spear.

Then Eitri put gold in the forge, and Brokk began to work the bellows again. The fly came back, but this time it sat on Brokk's chest and bit even harder. Brokk did feel it this time, but he did not stop working. Eitri took out his next masterpiece—long, beautiful, golden strings.

Finally, Eitri put iron in the forge, and Brokk began working the bellows again. This time the fly flew straight to his forehead and bit so hard that blood dripped into Brokk's eyes. Since he couldn't see, Brokk had to stop working the bellows for a second to wipe off the blood. Eitri took his final creation out of the forge—a mighty, forceful hammer. But because Brokk had to stop the bellows for a time because he couldn't see, the handle on the hammer was a little short.

The dwarfs went to Odin and presented their creations. The king of the gods looked at them and praised them. The dwarfs gave Odin the spear, the golden strings to Sif to use as hair, and the hammer to Thor. They had won the bet. "We will have Loki's head as our prize!" they cried.

"You'll have to catch me first," Loki said, and he took the shape of an eagle and flew high into the sky.

"Don't let him get away!" Brokk cried. Thor, the mighty thunder god, flew after Loki and grabbed him by his leg.

Now, Loki pleaded to Odin. "The dwarfs did *not* win the bet," he said. "They failed at their task. The hammer's shaft is short." And Odin agreed that this was true. The trickster god, in the form of a fly, had gotten the best of the dwarfs. They could not have Loki's head.

But before Loki could rejoice at his victory, Odin said one more thing: "The dwarfs can sew Loki's mouth together so that he learns his lesson!" So Eitri called on his cousins to sew Loki's lips shut. That is how Sif got her hair back and how Loki lost his voice.

HUMANS AND THE
FIRST WAR

One day, as the sons of Burr walked along the beach, they came across two pieces of driftwood. "Let's turn these pieces of wood into living beings," said the sons of Burr, and so they did. Odin gave them spirit, Vili gave them life, and Ve gave them fate. The two pieces of driftwood came to life and were named Ask and Embla. They built a farm in Middle Earth, which lies near Asgard, the home of the gods. And that is how humans were created by the gods.

There was peace for a long time after the gods created humans. The gods married Jotnar and elves. Some even married humans, and that is how the ancient heroes were born. It was a golden era, and the gods held their councils, played sports, and feasted at Idavoll, the eternal plains.

But then, one day, the elf-princess Gullveig came to the gods. She was beautiful but devious, and she knew powerful magic. She tricked the gods into promising that the goddess Heid would marry a particularly mean-spirited Jotun named Am. Heid went to live with Am, but she was miserable. She used a falcon to send word to the gods, telling them that she was being mistreated by Am and that he wouldn't let her see her family.

The gods gathered on the plains on Idavoll and discussed how to help Heid. Thor rose up and asked, "Who has betrayed the gods? Who tricked us into giving Heid to this horrible Jotun?" When he learned that it was Gullveig, he insisted on punishing her for her treachery. Three times the gods tried to burn Gullveig, but three times she survived.

Now the gods understood that only Heid's good magic could defeat Gullveig, and so Loki was sent to bring Heid back. He used his trickery to sneak Heid out of Am's great hall, but when the Jotnar found out, they chased Loki and Heid all the way to Idavoll. They believed that Heid belonged to them now, and they weren't going to give her back without a fight. A horde of angry Jotnar trampled the holy plains of the gods. Then Odin flung his spear, called Gungnir, into the Jotnar's army.

This was the beginning of the first war of the world.

Thor burst out of the ranks of the gods' army and went berserk. He swung his hammer, called Mjollnir, high above his head, smashing the Jotnar's skulls wherever he hit. Odin dove into the battle like a wolf, howling in his bloodthirst. Frey swung his mighty sword, and Freya flew on her falcon wings with a host of Valkyries. The battle was fierce, and much blood was spilled on Idavoll.

Finally, the gods and the Jotnar called a truce and agreed to exchange hostages. The humans Thjalfi and Roskva were sent to the gods and became Thor's servants. In return, the gods Mimir and Honir were sent to the Jotnar. The Jotnar thought that Honir would be a good king, so they elected him to rule over their homeland of Jotunheim. But Honir did not know how to rule. Every time the Jotnar asked him what to do, he said that they should ask Mimir instead. Mimir was wise and smart, and he had answers, but the Jotnar were angry. They felt betrayed, so they cut off Mimir's head and sent it back to Odin. Odin mourned the death of Mimir. He took Mimir's head, embalmed it with herbs and ointment, and spoke the ancient song-magic, *galdr*, over it. This brought Mimir's head back to life, and now, he and Odin talk about many mysteries of the world together.

When the gods saw all the blood that had been spilled on Idavoll during the war, they decided that they needed a big, strong wall to protect their homeland of Asgard. They searched far and wide for someone who could build it, until they found a man called the Masterbuilder. The gods asked the Masterbuilder what he wanted in return for his work on the wall, and he said that his payment should be the sun and the moon and to marry Freya, the goddess of love and war. It was a big request. The gods sat down at their thrones on Idavoll and held a council. After much talk, Loki advised them to agree to the deal. When the gods asked him what would happen when they no longer had the sun and the moon and Freya, Loki answered, "I have a plan!" So, the gods agreed to the Masterbuilder's terms, but they said that he would have to finish his work in one winter. The Masterbuilder accepted their terms.

The Masterbuilder began working in the late summer. Each day his horse, named Svadilfari, hauled giant boulders, which the Masterbuilder stacked higher and higher, until they reached the sky. The work progressed quickly, and when the gods realized that he might be done before Jul, the time of the high winter, they discussed what to do next. They were going to lose the sun and the moon and even Freya to this man. Thor rose up and said, "Loki, now it is time for your plan! What do you have in mind?" "Don't worry," Loki said. "I have an idea that will get our wall *and* let us keep the sun, the moon, and Freya."

The next day, the Masterbuilder worked as usual. His horse hauled boulders, and he stacked them. But, when evening came, the horse became distracted. Svadilfari saw a beautiful mare, white and shining, at the edge of the woods. She was running around, prancing and whinnying. Svadilfari tore his reigns and ran after her with the Masterbuilder on his heels. The two horses frolicked and played all night, with the Masterbuilder running behind them and yelling at Svadilfari to get back to work. Svadilfari did not listen to his master. Instead, Svadilfari and the mare disappeared in the woods, and the work on the wall stood still all through Jul.

Eventually, Svadilfari came back and the Masterbuilder continued his work, but he had lost precious time. Three days before spring, there was still a large portion of the wall missing. The Masterbuilder went to the gods and said that he could not finish the work before the end of winter. However, he said, "Since I have worked through winter, I should still be compensated. I want Freya's hand in marriage!" "No," Odin said, rising from his throne. "The deal was that you would only get paid if you completed the wall before the end of winter, and you have failed."

Odin's response angered the Masterbuilder greatly. He flew into a rage, and as he did so, his body and his face began to shift. The Masterbuilder no longer looked like the man they had struck the deal with. In fact, he was a Jotun, an ogre sent to trick them, who had been disguised all along! Thor quickly swung his hammer, Mjollnir, smashing the Masterbuilder's skull so that it shattered across the world and became all the little pebbles that lie on the ground. The gods did not have to give up the sun, the moon, or Freya, after all.

But here is what happened with Loki: He was not seen for 12 months after that evening when the mare lured Svadilfari into the woods.

Next year, in the late winter, Loki returned to the gods and brought an eight-legged foal with him. Loki gave the young stallion, black and beautiful, to Odin, and he was called Sleipnir. The wall was still unfinished, but the gods discovered that Sleipnir had enough strength even as a young foal to haul the same size boulders as Svadilfari. With Sleipnir's help, Thor finished the work that the disguised Jotun had begun. And Odin keeps his eight-legged horse Sleipnir with him to this very day.

ODIN,
RULER OF THE GODS

din was the ruler of the gods because he was the oldest. He was called All-father because he was the father of so many of the younger gods. He was also called the Father of the Slain because he cared like a father for many of the warriors who fell in battle. Odin lived in Valhall, the Hall of the Slain, which stood tall and bright under Yggdrasill, the world tree. Wolves lingered around Valhall, and birds of prey hovered above it. The roof was made of shields, and the walls are made of spears.

Inside this mighty hall, all the dead warriors sat on benches strewn with armor. Odin sat in his throne, which was called Hlidskjalf, along with two ravens, Huginn and Muninn. Every day, the ravens flew out over the world with messages from their master. It was said that Huginn was Odin's thought and Muninn was his memory. The warriors who understood the ravens' speech were called *berserkir* and *ulfhednar*— bear-warriors and wolf-warriors who used the strengths of bears and the fierceness of wolves in battle. These warriors could call upon Odin whenever they needed him to appear and throw his spear, Gungnir, over the army that he had chosen to join him in Valhall. The army that Odin threw his spear over would always perish.

Odin was also the god of wisdom, poetry, magic, and the runes. His desire to know everything in the world led him to sacrifice one of his eyes in exchange for such wisdom. To learn the runes, he hanged himself on the world tree, stabbed by a spear, without food or water, for nine nights. There was very little he didn't know—he even knew magic.

Freya taught Odin magic in the beginning of time, and he often did magic on the island of Samso, which lies in the Danish sea. Odin went to a place on Samso called Onshog, which means "Odin's Mound," and beat his drum. Odin knew the song-magic called *galdr*, the staff-magic called *gandr*, and another kind of magic called *seidr*, which could be used to travel between the worlds. He could turn himself into any kind of animal: a fish, a snake, a bird, or a wolf. He was also the god of the *volur*, the ancient priestesses of the Vikings. Odin's *galdr* could be used for healing, and his runes could be used to make weapons blunt, break shackles, stop flying arrows, and harm any enemy. In the beginning of time, Odin taught these tricks to his favored warriors and the ancient heroes.

One night, Odin's son Balder dreamt that he would die. The gods believed that dreams predicted the future, so this dream was very concerning. Odin went to Niflheim, the world of the dead, to consult with Hel, the goddess of the dead. He rode his horse Sleipnir through dark and deep valleys until he came to a world with no stars, no sun, and no moon. Then he crossed the river Gjoll and rode toward the north and then down. Finally, he came to the gates of Hel, called Nagrind.

A large black dog with a bloody neck was shackled in front of the gate, guarding it. Odin used his magic to tame the dog, and then he entered. He approached Hel in her mighty, dark hall.

"Who are you?" asked Hel.

Odin bowed and said, "My name is Way-tired, son of Battle-tired. I come to ask about my son, Balder. He has had a troubling dream. Is he going to die?"

Hel stretched out her arm and pointed with her shriveled finger to a table decked with fine cloth, silverware, and a horn for drinking from. A beautiful shield hung above the seat. She said, "Yes. Balder will soon dine here, killed by his own brother, Hother. And you, Odin, will fall before the wolf!"

Odin knew this meant that he, too, would die. He rode back to Valhall in a panic, but he did not stay there long. He believed that he could prevent his downfall by having more sons, so he jumped on Sleipnir and rode deep into Jotunheim. He befriended a Jotun named Grid, and nine months later, she gave birth to their son, Vidar.

Then Odin sought out Rind, an elf-princess in the East. She lived in a beautiful castle surrounded by high walls. Odin waited until nightfall below the balcony where her room was. It was a warm summer evening, so Rind came out to see the sunset. Then Odin spoke these words: "A creaking bow, a crackling flame, a gaping wolf, a croaking crow, a rootless tree, a swelling wave, a bubbling pot, a flying arrow, last night's ice, a tightly wound snake, a broken blade, a bear's play, a sick calf, a wizard's talk, a fresh-killed corpse, a field sown too early: Don't trust any of them, nor a son too soon. Weather creates crops, but wits make a son. Fair talk and fine gifts will win the woman's love. The one who woos will win!"

Rind knew Odin was saying that he was interested in her, but she wasn't sure if she was interested in him. "You cannot be here right now," she told him. "You must come back when it is fully dark." And so he did. But when he returned, he saw a band of warriors, armed with swords and torches, marching under Rind's balcony.

Odin came back again, close to the morning. Now the warriors were gone, and he climbed the balcony. As he slipped into Rind's room, he saw her bed, and there, right on the bed, stood an angry, ugly, old dog. Rind was nowhere to be found. The dog barked at Odin, so he was forced to run once more.

But Odin would not give up. He dressed himself as an old woman and went to Rind's castle one last time. Passing himself off as an old nurse, Odin finally got to meet Rind. He spoke to her under his veil, and when she realized that it was him in disguise, she fell back laughing. He told her how he ran from the warriors and the old, mangy dog in her room, and she laughed even harder. "I sent the warriors and the dog as a test of your devotion," Rind said, "and you passed." They spoke all night until the first morning light. From then on, they spent much time together.

After some time, Rind give birth to their son, whom they named Bui. Rind taught Bui all the skills of a good warrior. In time, as Hel had foretold, Odin's son Balder was killed, and so Bui swore that he would not cut his hair until he had avenged the death of his brother Balder.

Soon after this, Odin returned home to Asgard. The gods laughed when they heard how difficult it had been to win the love of Rind. Loki, especially, liked to tease him about it, but in the back of their minds, all the gods knew that when brothers start fighting each other, the end of the world—Ragnarok—is not far away.

FRIGG,
GODDESS OF THE MARSHES

rigg was the goddess of the marshes. It is said that Frigg knew everything, but she rarely told anyone what she knew. She lived in Fensalir, the great marsh-halls, with her 12 maidens. There was Saga, the warden of stories; Eir, the goddess of healing; Gefiun, the warden of virgins; and Fulla, Frigg's trusted servant. Siofn, the goddess of love, and Lofn, the goddess of unions, were sent out by Frigg to make people fall in love. Var listened to people's oaths and protected private agreements between lovers, but Vor was wise and curious, and she saw to it that women always found out what they need to know. Syn guarded all doors and made sure that no one could enter where they were not wanted. Hlin protected anyone that Frigg wanted shielded from harm, and Snotra was the goddess of knowledge. And the last of the 12 was Gna, who rode her horse across sky and sea, delivering messages from Frigg.

Frigg was Odin's wife, and together they had three sons: Balder, Hother, and Hermoder. Frigg always favored Balder—as did Nanna, a goddess who dreamed of marrying him someday. Odin, on the other hand, favored Hother.

When Balder and Hother were young boys, Odin and Frigg were sitting on Odin's throne, which is called Hlidskjalf, looking out across the world. They saw the two boys fishing, and Frigg said to Odin, "I bet you that Balder catches the biggest fish."

Odin replied, "That might be true, but I bet you that Hother becomes king before Balder."

Unfortunately, the wind caught the brothers' boat, and it drifted far out to sea. The next morning, it had reached the other side of the ocean, and Balder and Hother went ashore. There they found a small, modest hut where an old woman and an old man were living. The elderly couple took the brothers in and let them stay for the winter. When spring arrived, the brothers took their boat back home.

When the brothers finally arrived back on their own land, Hother jumped ashore and kicked the boat back out to sea, shouting, "Go where the trolls take you, brother!" Hother went back to his parents and was welcomed while Balder drifted back out to sea. Hother soon became king, just as his father predicted, but Balder was nowhere to be seen. Believing that she would never see her childhood love again, Nanna married Hother.

In her distress over her lost son, Frigg went out across the world and took oaths from all things, living and dead, asking them not to harm Balder should they cross paths with him. The trees agreed, the rocks agreed, the sea, the wind, the flowers, the sky, the birds, the animals, the fish, the snakes—even the dwarfs and the Jotnar—agreed.

Meanwhile, Hother ruled his kingdom, but he was a selfish king. He did not treat his guests well, and many left his house hungry. Frigg said to Odin, "Look at your boy Hother! He treats his guests poorly and lets them leave his hall hungry."

Odin knew it was true but said, "What are you going to do about it now? He's the king!"

Frigg sent Gna, her messenger, to visit Hother while he was asleep. In Hother's dream, Gna told him, "Beware that you do not get bewitched by a wizard—he has come to this land, and he walks the roads in tattered clothing. Not even the meanest dog will attack him!"

Hother woke up in a sweat from his dream and ordered that his fiercest dogs be put outside the gate. Not long after, a man came walking by in tattered clothing. The fierce dogs that always barked and jumped at everyone else let him pass. Hother knew that this was the visitor Gna had warned him about, so he had the man seized and shackled and put him between two fires to torture him for nine days. "You will not bewitch me," Hother told the man.

After nine days, Nanna came to the great hall and saw the man placed between the fires. When the man saw Nanna, he said, "Flames! You're burning hot! Fire, get away from me! My cloak is singed, my cape is burning before my eyes!"

Nanna took pity on the man. She gave him a drink from a mead horn. Then he said, "For nine nights I have been sitting between these flames, without food, without water. No one offered me anything, except Nanna. Now she alone shall rule the lands of the Goths, from Hreid's Sea to Hrimnir's Gate."

As soon as Hother and Nanna heard these words, they realized who the shackled stranger was: It was Balder!

Frigg ran into the great hall, delighted to finally have her son home. Hother leapt up and released Balder, but the bond of brotherhood had been broken between them, and Balder demanded his revenge. So they agreed to meet in *holmgang*, the ancient custom of duel, on the eternal plains of Idavoll.

On the day of the duel, both Hother and Balder came to Idavoll with great armies. Loki stood at the edge of the plain, watching. He was never really fond of Balder. He found Frigg sitting in her hall, Fensalir, and he approached her in the disguise of an old woman.

"What is happening at Idavoll?" Frigg asked the old woman. "How fares my son?"

Loki, disguised as the old woman, replied, "Balder is unharmed so far."

Frigg nodded. "Weapons and stone will not hurt my Balder. Over the years that he's been missing, I received oaths from them all."

Still disguised as the old woman, Loki raised his eyebrows. "Has everything in the whole world taken an oath from you not to harm Balder?"

Frigg replied, "Almost everything. There grows a tree west of Valhall, a sturdy ash, and it seemed to me that this tree would be least likely to harm Balder, so I did not seek an oath from it."

Upon hearing that, Loki turned into a bird and flew out of the marshes, back to Idavoll, to the tree called Yggdrasill, the world tree. He broke off a branch. Then he went to Hother, the brother he favored, who was standing at the edge of Idavoll. Loki handed Hother the arrow he had fashioned from the branch and said, "Shoot this arrow at your brother if you wish to win."

Suddenly, the banging of the shields stopped. Everyone fell silent. Balder took his sword and advanced on the plain, but Hother put the arrow in his bow and shot it from a great distance.

The arrow swished through the air and struck Balder right in the heart. He fell dead on the plain. All the gods stood there; they didn't have the strength to lift Balder up. When they tried to speak, no words came out, only weeping.

Finally, Frigg spoke and asked who was going to avenge Balder's death. This was the moment that Odin's son Bui had been fated for from birth. Bui stepped out of the crowd and said, "I will."

Bui and Hother fell on each other that day on Idavoll. Bui succeeded in avenging the death of Balder, sending Hother and his army to Hel. This fight among brothers was the greatest tragedy of them all.

Hermoder's
Ride to Hel

fter Balder was killed by his brother, the gods carried his body to the sea. They placed Balder's body on his ship, the biggest ship of them all. The gods summoned the troll-woman Hyrrokkin to perform Balder's funeral ceremony. She came riding in on a wolf, using vipers as reins.

The gods placed food, golden cups of mead, and many other precious items on the ship with Balder. Horses, dogs, and birds were carried on there, too. Odin laid his precious ring, Draupnir, on the pyre. When Nanna saw this, her heart burst with sorrow. She died instantly of heartbreak, and so the gods placed her on the ship next to Balder to rest in peace.

Thor lifted the troll-woman Hyrrokkin up onto the ship. She said, "I see beyond the threshold. I see into Niflheim, the world of the dead. There I see my kin, and I see Balder seated in the great hall, feasting with his brother, reunited and at peace with each other at last." Then

Hyrrokkin cut the head off a rooster, which had a body as dark as soot and neck as red as blood. She threw the head away and placed its body in the boat. With that, Hyrrokkin lit the ship on fire. Soon, it was engulfed in flames. This was how a Norse funeral was held, and the gods thought to themselves, *Balder will have a good journey to Niflheim.*

But Frigg was not ready to say goodbye to her son, no matter how peaceful his journey. She wanted him back. So she asked her youngest son, Hermoder the Bold, to go to Hel on her behalf to offer a ransom and return with the brothers. Odin brought out his horse, the eight-legged stallion, Sleipnir, and said to Hermoder, "Here, my boy. It is time to ride across the dewy mountains, through the ogres' lands, to Hel. I'll give you my horse to carry you over the dark, flickering flames, through the deep valleys of death."

Hermoder spoke to Sleipnir, "Carry us across the world and through the darkness, and let us return, or I fear that we shall both become victims of that mean old ogress Hel." Then they galloped away.

Hermoder rode for nine nights, through deep and dark valleys. He saw no stars, no moon, and no sun for all that time. Finally, he came to the river Gjoll and crossed a golden bridge. On the other side, the guardian of the bridge, Modgud, was awaiting him. "Who are you?" she asked. "The other day, a whole army of bloody warriors with ice in their hair and beards rode over this bridge, but the bridge trembles more under your horse's hoofs. You do not look like you're dead."

Hermoder replied, "Indeed, I am not dead. I have been sent by Frigg and Odin to barter with Hel. I am going to retrieve my brother Balder from Niflheim."

Modgud nodded and told him, "Balder passed the river Gjoll and rode over the golden bridge not so long ago. You will have to ride toward the north and then down to find Nagrind, the gates of Hel."

Hermoder rode on. When he reached the gates of Hel, they were so high and icy that he could not pass. So he performed Odin's *galdr* (song-magic) and awoke a Valkyrie, or war goddess, named Sigrdrifa. The Valkyrie rose from the ground and said, "I've slept for long. I've slumbered too much. Great are the misfortunes of men. Odin is the reason that I could not break the sleep. He covered me with shields in Skati's Grove. He lit the enemy of wood on fire around my hall, in a blaze, and told the warrior to cross it. He told the fearless to wake me from my sleep. The fine spoiler of gold came to me. He alone is better than all the others, a Danish Viking in the army! Come now, Hermoder, and I shall lead you to Hel. Take my hand and we shall cross to Niflheim."

Hermoder knew that this Valkyrie would help him. Together, they went through Nagrind, the gates of Hel, and into the courtyard. There, in the land of the dead, Hermoder saw many awful things: skeletons and ghosts, ghouls and dead men. He and Sigrdrifa walked along a river filled with swords and spears, axes, and all kinds of weaponry. "This is the river Slith," Sigrdrifa told him. "It will burst out of Niflheim someday, when the world is destroyed."

After walking a long time, they entered a great hall. Hermoder looked to the left and then to the right. He saw benches made of iron and sitting on them were many Draugar—the undead, the ghosts. At the end of the hall, he saw Hel on her throne. Beside her were Geirrod, the evil ogre-king, and his two daughters, Gjalp and Greip. Geirrod had a huge iron rod sticking out from his chest, and his daughters' backs were broken from a battle they'd had with Thor long ago.

On the walls in Hel's hall, there were beautiful drinking horns, shields, and weapons. Hermoder was impressed with their splendor, but Sigrdrifa said, "Don't touch them. If you do, you will have to stay here forever. Don't take anything that Hel offers you, because then you won't escape with your life."

Hermoder approached Hel. In front of her sat Hanginkjapta, an ogress with a broken jaw that hung down to her chest. Hanginkjapta spoke for Hel. First, she offered Hermoder a drink of mead, but, remembering Sigrdrifa's advice, he declined. Then the servant Ganglot came toward him, her left foot broken and dragging along the floor. She offered him some food. Hermoder saw that the food was rotten and moldy and declined.

Then, Hermoder saw Balder and his love Nanna seated in thrones across from the ogre-king Geirrod. Hermoder fell to his knee and begged Hel to let them go. She did not move, but her voice came roaring from the mouth of Hanginkjapta: "If all things in the world, alive and dead, weep for Balder, then he will return to the gods. But if one thing, alive or dead, refuses to weep, then he will stay here."

Hermoder was dismissed. Balder and Nanna followed him out of the hall, but they stopped outside. As long as they remained dead, they could not go any further. As a token to remember him by, Balder gave Hermoder the ring, Draupnir, to return to Odin. Now that Draupnir had been to Niflheim, it would drip and produce a new golden ring every ninth night. Nanna gave Hermoder a swan-cloak for Frigg and a golden ring for Fulla, and then they parted ways.

Sigrdrifa guided Hermoder safely back to Nagrind, but when they got there, he could not pass through the gate. So Sigrdrifa took a rooster, which had a bloodred neck and soot-dark body, cut its head off, and threw it over the gate. Immediately, Hermoder heard a rooster croaking on the other side, and sunlight shone through the mist. In an instant, he was back in the world of the living.

Hermoder rode home to Asgard and told the gods what Hel had said—that when everyone and everything wept for Balder, he would be released. Upon hearing this, Frigg and her 12 maidens flew across the world as swans for days and days and asked all things, dead and alive, to weep for Balder. Everyone agreed. Except for a single troll.

"What is your name?" Frigg asked the troll when she came upon her cave.

"My name is Thank You," replied the troll.

"Will you weep for my son?" asked Frigg.

The troll replied, "Thank You weeps only dry tears for Balder's death. I got no goods or favors from the old man's son, dead or alive. Let Hel keep what she's got!"

Because of that lone troll, Balder still has not been released. Legend has it that Frigg eventually struck a deal with Hel. Hel promised that after Ragnarok, after the end of the world, she will release Balder to his loving mother, Frigg.

THOR,
GOD OF THUNDER

hor—the son of Odin and Jord, the goddess of the earth—was the strongest of the gods and often called *midgards verjandi*, Protector of Middle Earth. Thor controlled the rain and thunder, and with that, he controlled the crops in the fields. He was known for being a skilled and strong warrior who fought the Jotnar and went on raids in the East.

But Thor was not just a mighty god, he was also a loving and caring god. Many went to him for protection against illnesses, and he was a great guide for seafarers. In ancient times, when the Scandinavians went to Iceland, many of them believed they were guided by Thor.

For example, a Viking named Thorolf settled near a mountain in Iceland that he called Helgafell, which means "holy mountain." He dedicated the mountain to Thor to thank him for his guidance and protection. Back in Norway, Thorolf had a temple where he worshipped Thor, and when he decided to leave for Iceland, he took with him his god-pillar, a tall wooden post he had carved Thor's face on. When he came within sight of Iceland, he threw the pillar overboard and said that he would make a home wherever it landed.

In Asgard, Thor's home was called Thrudheim, and it was a place of great power. He was married to Sif, and their daughter was Thrud. She was a much desired young goddess. Both the dwarfs and the Jotnar tried to woo her.

Thor's hammer was called Mjollnir, which means "the grinder." It was a mighty weapon, and when he threw it, it always hit its target and return to his hand. Thor wore metal gloves and a belt of metal called Megingjord. He often rode his chariot, driven by two goats: Tanngniost (which means "tooth grinder") and Tanngnist (which means "tooth crusher"). When Thor's chariot rolled over the sky, the heavenly vault trembled and rumbled—that is the thunder that we humans hear in Middle Earth. When Thor's hammer struck, sparks flew across the sky—that is the lightning that we humans see in Middle Earth. When thunder cracks and lightning strikes, you can be sure that Thor is out hunting trolls, ogres, and Jotnar.

There was no one in this world who is wise enough to know all Thor's adventures, but one of the best-known myths is about how Thor lost his hammer, Mjollnir. One day, Thor woke up, and after stretching and yawning, he reached out for his hammer. Then he discovered that it was gone!

He searched all over in Thrudheim, but Mjollnir was nowhere to be seen. His beard began to shake, and his red locks tossed around his head. Then he turned to Loki and growled, "Have you seen my hammer? Where might it be? The god has been robbed of his weapon!"

Loki quickly recognized the stern stare in Thor's eyes and knew that something had to be done. He slipped out as fast as he could, and once outside, his arms turned into wings and his feet into a feathery tail.

With a bash of his wings, Loki made a storm wind across the world as he flew straight to Jotunheim.

After a long journey, Loki came to the farm of Thrym, the Lord of Ogres. Thrym was sitting on a mound, stroking his horse's mane, and playing with golden rings. Thrym saw Loki and asked him, "Why are you here among the Jotnar, Loki? You do not belong here."

"Have you hidden Thor's hammer?" Loki demanded.

"Maybe I have, maybe I haven't," said Thrym, "but anyone who wants it must dig eight leagues down into the ground and give me Thrud's hand in marriage. Only then will Thor, Fire-rider, get his hammer back!"

Then Loki turned around in the air, the feathers on his back whirring, and returned home to Asgard. Thor nervously asked, "What news do you have for me, Loki?"

Loki replied, "Thrym has hidden your hammer deep below the ground, and he wants your daughter Thrud's hand in marriage, or he'll keep the hammer for himself!"

Quickly, the two gods ran to Thrud's hall and stormed inside. Thor called to his daughter, "Thrud, put on a veil and put some color on your cheeks and lips. We must ride to Jotunheim!"

Thrud looked at him in disbelief. Then she understood that he was serious, and her beautiful face lit up in laughter. She laughed so hard that all of Thrudheim shook. "You must think that I'm a fool if you believe that I'll go with you to marry an ogre!" But Thor persisted and Thrud grew angry. She said, "Fix your own problem, father! I'm not yours—nor any man's—to barter with!"

Soon, all the gods were gathered in Thrudheim, discussing what to do. Then the god Heimdall spoke with a spark in his eye, "Put Thor in that bridal veil and give him the brilliant Brising's necklace! Have keys dangling on his chest and a dress falling on his knees! Let us adorn his head with style, gems and all that."

Thor looked at them all in despair and said, "Ahem, I think my manhood will be hit the hardest from that."

But Loki interrupted him, "Shut your mouth, Thor! The Jotnar will trample our plains again if we don't solve this problem."

And so, it came to be that Thor dressed up as his daughter Thrud, with a bridal veil and Brising's necklace on his chest. Loki dressed up as his maid, and together they made the journey to Thrym's halls in Jotunheim.

Thrym believed that Thrud had come to him, ready to wed him. He gave the disguised Thor the finest seat in his hall. At a splendid banquet, Thrym had oxen, salmon, bread, and mead brought out for the guests. Thor quickly gulped down a whole ox, then eight salmon, and 12 loaves of bread. He washed it down with no less than three caskets of mead.

Thrym said to the maid, "Have you ever seen a bride eat like that? I've never seen anyone eat so much and drink so much mead!"

Loki was clever and responded, "Thrud has been so excited to meet you that she hasn't eaten for days!"

Then Thrym leaned over to give the bride a kiss on the cheek, but the sight that met him made him jump back the whole length of the hall. He turned to the maid again and said, "Thrud's eyes are fierce. It seems that fire shoots out of them!"

Loki said, "Oh, she hasn't slept in days. She was so desperate to meet you!"

After the banquet, it was time for the wedding. Thrym commanded that the hammer Mjollnir be brought out to consecrate the ceremony: "Bring out the hammer to hallow the bride and groom in the name of Var!"

As soon as the ogre put Mjollnir down in Thor's lap, Thor's heart laughed in his chest. In that moment, Thrym, the Lord of Ogres, saw through Thor's disguise. He tried to cry out, "That is not Thrud under the veil!" but he was too late.

Quickly, Thor swung the hammer high, smacking Thrym the Thief right on his cheek. With a thunderclap and roaring laughter, Thor smashed his skull. Then he went berserk on all the other ogres there, large and small, until only Thor and Loki left Thrym's halls in one piece. And that is the story of what happens to those who try to steal from the strongest god.

LOKI,
THE TRICKSTER GOD

Loki, sometimes called Lopt, was the trickiest of the gods—good and bad and everything in between. He was a god of fire, air, and water, and he went between the worlds as he pleased. His father was Farbauti, an ancient Jotun, and his mother was Laufey, a beautiful goddess.

He was Odin's blood brother. Just like Odin, Loki could turn himself into any kind of animal. He knew Odin's magic and was just as skilled as the Ruler of the Gods.

The gods became fed up with Loki's antics when Balder was killed. When they discovered that Loki had given Hother the arrow that killed Balder, the gods were furious. They wanted to punish Loki, but he escaped from them and wandered the wilderness for a long time.

One day, Loki was walking along a river and came upon a house close to a waterfall. It belonged to a wizard named Hreidmar. Loki went into the house and said, "Hello to those who sit on the benches! I have come from far away. A guest needs water, a dry towel, and a fire to sit by."

Hreidmar welcomed him and gave him a seat by the fire. He offered his guest water and food, and they began talking. Hreidmar quickly discovered whom he was talking to, and in the back of his mind, he began to devise a plan. He had heard the gods were looking for Loki, so Hreidmar thought that he could get a nice prize for catching him.

When Loki went to sleep, Hreidmar planned to kill him with an axe. But Loki was smart and knew that he was in danger, so instead of lying in his bed, he put a log under the sheets and slept under the bed. Later that night, the door opened and Hreidmar came in. Loki heard a loud *thud* and a *crack* when the axe hit the log. Hreidmar thought that he had split Loki's skull, so he went back to bed, intending to collect the body in the morning and bring it to the gods.

Once he knew Hreidmar was fast asleep, Loki changed shape to an otter and slipped out of a window. He climbed down to the waterfall and jumped into the water. There he caught a fat salmon, and, in the morning, he feasted on it while sitting on a boulder.

When dawn broke, Hreidmar discovered that it was a log, not Loki, under the sheets in the bed. He went out of his house and used his magic sight to look for the god. Soon, he realized that the otter on the boulder by the waterfall was Loki. He powerfully threw a rock that knocked Loki out. Then he took the otter back home and skinned it.

Loki fell out of the otter's skin onto the floor. "Please, friend," he begged. "Do not kill me, and do not return me to the gods."

"You are my prisoner," Hreidmar told Loki. "If you want to escape with your life, you must cover this otter's skin in gold."

"I will do as you ask," Loki promised.

Loki changed his shape to a pike and jumped back into the river. He swam down into a cave and found the dwarf Andvari, who was living there in the shape of a trout. Loki convinced Andvari to open his rock full of gold. After he had taken enough gold to cover the otter's skin, Loki demanded Andvari's ring that he used to multiply his gold. Andvari gave Loki the ring, but cursed it when Loki left, saying that destruction would befall anyone who kept it.

Loki went back to Hreidmar and covered the otter's skin in gold, as promised. He intended to keep the ring for himself, but Hreidmar complained that one otter whisker had not been turned to gold, so he made Loki give up the ring, too. Loki escaped with his life, but not long after, Hreidmar, now the owner of the cursed ring, was killed by his own son.

When Loki left Hreidmar's home, he knew he needed to guard himself better because he wouldn't be safe anywhere he went. He spoke a *galdr* verse and created a magic reindeer from the plants growing around him. The head was made of spruce, the horns of naked willows, the feet were made of rushes, the legs of reeds from the lake, and its veins were of withered weeds. Daisies from the meadows became its eyes, water flowers were used for ears, and rough fir bark became its skin. He used sappy wood for its muscles and hard oak for its teeth. Then Loki rode away on his magic reindeer, crossing the evergreen woods and the naked taiga—the snow forest.

Finally, when Loki was the farthest away that he could get, he set up a small tent with four openings so that he could see all the four corners of the world. In the daytime, Loki lived in the river in the shape of a salmon, and in the evenings, he came back to his tent in his human form. He grew so bored living on his own that he began making many things. He carved little figures and made art. He also made tools and new inventions.

One evening, Loki was sitting in his tent, tying strings together in little squares to make a net, when he heard a mighty clash. It was Thor, riding across the sky. The gods had finally found him! With Thor came Odin, Vidar, Freya, Frey, Skadi, Njord, Tyr, and all the other gods. Loki threw the net he had made into the fire, quickly changed shape to a salmon, and jumped into the river.

When the gods entered the tent, Thor saw the shape of the burnt net in the ashes, and he understood that it could be used to catch fish. The gods worked together to quickly make such a net, and then they went to the river.

Thor held one end of the net while the other gods held the other end, and they dragged it through the water, looking for Loki. But Loki was clever and squeezed down between the rocks. Then the gods threw the net out once more, and this time they held it down, closer to the bottom of the river. Then Loki leapt over the net and up the waterfall. Thor saw the salmon and, despite the fish form, knew it to be Loki.

The gods divided into two groups, each holding an end of the net, while Thor waded in the water in front of the net to make Loki swim toward the sea. Loki knew that the sea was too dangerous for him, so once again, he tried to jump over the net. He threw himself over it and jumped as high as he could, but Thor was in the middle of the river, and he reached out to catch Loki. He caught the fish with his strong fist, clasping around the salmon's body. It was slick, so Thor's hand slipped to the end of the tail, which is why the salmon now tapers at its tail.

At last, Loki would be punished for his role in Balder's death. The gods shackled Loki to a rock in the underworld and put a viper over his head. This viper drips venom from its mouth, but Loki's wife, Sigyn, held a bowl under its fangs, so that Loki didn't get the venom in his face. When Sigyn needed to empty the bowl, the venom dripped on Loki's face, and this made him tremble in such great pain that the earth shook. Vikings have always believed that Loki's trembling is the reason for earthquakes.

FREYA
AND BRISING'S NECKLACE

reya was considered the most beautiful of the goddesses, with golden hair like amber and lips red like blood. The title *frua*, which is given to women of honor, comes from her name. Freya had many other names, too: Mardol, Horn, Syr, and Gefn. Freya was both a lover and a fighter, and it is said that if you wish to pray for love, you should pray to her. Fierce in battle, she was the Lady of the Shield-maidens and lived in a land called Folkvangar, the army-fields, in her great hall, Sessrumnir. Half of all the slain warriors sat with her there; the other half of the slain warriors sat with Odin in Valhall.

Freya was fond of treasures and, for that reason, Vikings would offer gold to her in their temples. Her most prized possession was a piece of jewelry called Brising's necklace, but keeping something so beautiful safe was not easy.

A long time ago, Freya was traveling in Sweden, and to disguise herself, she used the name Gefn. One day she came to the castle of

the Swedish king Gylfi. Gefn spoke to Gylfi and asked him if she could have a plot of land. Gylfi agreed, on one condition. He said, "You can only have as much as you can plow around in one day." Gefn agreed and then turned into a falcon and flew far north to the Finnmark—the northernmost parts of Scandinavia—where she lived with the dwarf Brising. In time, Gefn and Brising had four sons: Dvalinn, Alfrik, Berling, and Grer.

Soon after, Gefn returned to Gylfi and said that she was ready to claim her land. Then she took her four sons and sang *galdr* over them, turning them into giant oxen. With her four oxen, she drew the plough so deep that it buried itself under the landmass. The oxen pulled so hard that steam rose from their backs. They cut a furrow deep enough to become a large river, and then they drew it into a ring and uprooted the land. This land became the Danish island called Zealand, and the hole the oxen made became the Swedish lake called Malar.

Now that Gefn had her own land, she sailed it toward the south of Sweden, which is where Zealand is today. When she gave the land to her four sons, they were so grateful that they made her a golden necklace called Brising's necklace. It was the most beautiful piece of jewelry ever seen. Some said that it shone as bright as the sun.

When Freya returned to Asgard with Brising's necklace, Loki couldn't contain his greed. He was so taken with the beautiful piece of jewelry that he thought he must have it. One night, when Freya was sound asleep in her home, Sessrumnir, Loki turned into a little flea, jumped up on the door handle, and squeezed through a slit in the wood. On the other side of the door, he turned into a little mouse, thinking that he would be able to carry the necklace out on his back.

Unfortunately for him, Freya is the Lady of Cats, so the little mouse found itself chased around the room by Freya's two hungry black cats. Luckily, Loki found a little hole in the wall where he could hide. Once the cats got tired of waiting for him to come out, he changed shape to a snake and slid over the floor to the chest where Freya had put Brising's necklace. He then turned into a hawk, opened the lid with his talons, snatched the necklace, and flew out through the chimney.

When Freya awoke the next morning, she discovered that the necklace was gone. She rushed to Himinbjorg, Heimdall's home. Heimdall is known as the Watchman of the Gods because he has such good eyesight that he can see to the end of the world and such good hearing that he can hear the wool grow on the backs of sheep. If anyone could find the necklace, it was him.

Heimdall climbed the tallest cliff on his mountain, Himinbjorg, and from there he examined all the corners of the world. He called to Freya, "I see him! I see Loki! He is sitting by the end of the world in a hawk's nest, perched on a high cliff, not far from Niflheim." Then Heimdall turned himself into a bright white hawk and flew quickly toward Loki. When he came to the cliff where Loki was sitting and admiring the gold necklace, Heimdall dropped down on the Tricker of the Gods. He hit Loki so hard that he fell forward and dropped the necklace into the deep ocean.

"No!" Loki shouted. He quickly turned himself into a seal and leapt into the frozen waves. Heimdall took the shape of a walrus and followed him. Deep at the bottom of the sea, the brilliant Brising's necklace was lighting up the ocean floor. As soon as Loki saw it, he took it in his mouth and swiftly rushed to the surface, but Heimdall followed close behind and managed to hook his tusk in the chain. Heimdall pulled hard with his neck, swinging Loki out of the ocean, and landing them both on an island. Loki changed his shape again to a black moose and intended to run away, but Heimdall was right there behind him, now in the shape of a bear. The two gods fought fiercely. The battle raged on and off, back and forth, between them. Days went by, then months, and soon, they had been fighting for a whole year. Neither of them tired or backed down, and it is said that they fought for a total of 133 years.

Finally, after all that time passed, Freya found them. She appeared in the sky, flying on her falcon wings from the east with a host of Valkyries, the war goddesses. "Enough!" she shouted. Loki and Heimdall froze where they stood. A bright light shone behind Freya, and it seemed to them that she brought the dawning sun itself. Freya landed on the ground and turned into her common form. She walked up to them and said, "What will it take for you two to stop your fighting? What is the price for giving me back my necklace?"

Loki said, "Give me what you gave those dwarfs, then you can have your necklace!" He wanted land of his own, just as Freya had given to her sons. Loki stretched out his hand for Freya to shake in agreement. Freya paused for a long moment, then stretched her hand toward him.

But then she drew a knife from her belt and cut her finger so that the blood dripped down in Loki's hand. She bent down on one knee and filled her hand with dirt from Hjadningavik's soil and poured it over the blood. "There," she said, "now you've got what I gave those dwarfs: my blood and some dirt."

She then grabbed Brising's necklace in her falcon talons and flew high into the sky. She flew so far up that no one could follow her, and up there, far from the reach of greedy hands, she hung the shining necklace in the sky, and it became the light that we now call the morning star.

FREY,
THE GOD OF KINGS

n ancient times, Nordic kings believed they descended from the gods. Some were the descendants of Odin; others were the descendants of Frey, whose name means "lord." When he was little, Frey was given the elves' great hall, Alfheim, as a gift, which was why he was called the Lord of Elves. The god of fertility, Frey ruled the sunshine and the rain. Vikings would often dedicate their horses and their boars to him as an offering. Frey had a golden boar, which was made by the sons of Ivaldi—the same dwarfs that made Odin's spear, Gungnir. Frey's golden boar ran so fast that it flew across the sky.

One spring day, Frey came riding through the woods. All the leaves on the trees were shining green and golden in the sunlight. Then he saw seven swans fly over his head and land in a lake not far from where he was riding. The swans swam up to the shore, stepped up on a large rock, and took off their swan-coats, revealing that they were not swans at all but were in fact seven beautiful young women. For a time, they played in the water and sat and talked with one another on the rock. Frey was sitting in the bushes across the lake, very taken with their beauty.

Suddenly, one of the women looked up and said, "We are not alone." Quickly, they all put on their swan-coats and flew away. But one of them, the youngest, stopped before she flew away and turned around to meet eyes with Frey in the thicket on the other side. Frey went home to Alfheim, but he could not shake the sight of the beautiful eyes of that mysterious creature. He couldn't sleep. He couldn't eat. All he did was think of her. He had to find out who she was!

Frey went to his throne from where he could see the entire world and began searching for the young woman. He sat upon his throne for a long time, looking out across Earth. Then, in the distance, he saw a young woman walking across the courtyard in Middle Earth. The light of the sun's rays shone off her hair and her skin, and he knew that this was the young woman he sought.

He jumped on his golden boar and rode it across Middle Earth. When he finally came to the land where this woman lived, he used his *galdr* magic to turn the boar into a tree. He then put on a disguise and walked to the outskirts of the woman's castle, where he met a shepherd sitting on a mound, tending the sheep. Frey said, "Tell me, shepherd, how can I get to talk with the young woman who lives in that castle?"

The shepherd answered, "Are you doomed or dead? You'll never have a chance to talk to Gymir's wife!"

But Frey knew that he and this woman were destined to be together. He said, "In a single day my fate was made, and all my life was decided. I need to talk to her!" Ignoring the shepherd's warning, he went on across the fields and came to the castle.

"Who goes there?" asked a watchman from the tower.

"I am Frey, son of Njord, god of the seafarers. I have come to talk to the shining lady, the swan-woman who lives here."

"Are you stupid or just mad? She is the wife of Gymir, the king of these lands!" said the watchman. "You better just run off before he finds out what you're here for. He does not take kindly to folks like you!"

Knowing that he could not speak to the swan-woman just then, Frey went away from the castle and walked into town. He told people there that his name was Rig and was given lodging with many kind folks. Frey knew that a guest should not stay too long, so he only lived with the townspeople who welcomed him into their homes for a few days at a time. During his stay with three different couples, Frey taught them many skills and, in turn, he learned about Gymir's kingdom. The townspeople were poor and sad because Gymir was a greedy king. He demanded high taxes and overworked them.

Frey learned that many years ago, Gymir had gone to battle with a king named Volund and conquered his realm. After his victory, Gymir took King Volund and his daughters as slaves. He enslaved Volund by cutting Volund's tendons in his heels so that he couldn't walk. Volund was made to work gold every day, creating the great Grotti, a stone mill that made gold when someone churned it and spoke a verse. Gymir chained Volund's daughters, Fenja and Menja, to the Grotti and made them churn the mill day and night to make him rich. Gymir had also taken Gerd, Volund's third and most beautiful daughter, to be his wife. Gerd was not happy with Gymir, and it was said that her only joy was when she could sneak out of the castle's halls and use her elf powers to fly like a swan with the other elves.

Once a year, King Gymir held a great feast, and it was his custom to invite the people into his courtyard so they could gawk at all his riches. On the day of the great feast, all the townspeople, Frey included, came to the courtyard to look at all the splendor in the castle.

Soon, Gymir and his queen, Gerd, came out on the balcony. The townspeople were cheering for them, but in the middle of the crowd, Gerd spotted the same eyes that she had seen that day at the lake, and she understood who it was. She gave Frey a smile. He had found her!

When Gymir noticed Gerd looking at Frey, he raised his hand to stop the cheering. Then he pointed at Frey and shouted, "Take that man! Put him in shackles!"

Gymir's biggest warrior, Bele, rushed toward Frey to grab him, but Frey ducked and escaped the giant's claws. He ran over to a wall where the antlers of the deer Eikthyrnir were hanging. Eikthyrnir had been the largest deer in the world, and Gymir was very proud that he had killed it on a hunting trip. A fierce fight broke out between Frey and Bele. Frey used the dead deer's antlers to defend himself, and in the end he won.

As the giant's body lay in the middle of the courtyard, Gymir asked, "Who is this man that beat my best warrior?"

Frey replied, "It is me, Frey, son of Njord the god of the seafarers, Lord of Alfheim!" He threw off his cloak, and a bright light shone all around him. When Gymir saw the light, it was as if he melted like snow on a summer's day. Gymir was defeated!

After that, all the people were freed from Gymir's greedy reign. Frey cut the shackles off Fenja and Menja, and they pushed the Grotti into the sea, where it now lies at the bottom of the ocean. The mill continues to grind, but instead of creating gold, it creates salt, which is why seawater tastes salty. Frey then freed Volund and gave him eagle wings to compensate for his poor feet. Volund took over Gymir's kingdom, and there was peace and happiness during his reign. Frey and Gerd reunited, went home to Alfheim, and lived happily ever after.

Idun,
the Goddess of Youth

A long time ago, when the world was still young, the three gods—Odin, Honir, and Loki—were out walking, exploring what they had created. They crossed the great wilderness, went through the deep woods, trekked over the the snow forest, and scaled the tallest mountains.

Then they came to a valley, barren, cold, and rocky. There were only minor plants growing in the cracks between the cliffs, but to the gods' surprise, they found a herd of goats living there. Honir took his sling, put a decently sized rock in it, and flung it at a large black goat. The goat fell over dead on the spot. The three gods sat down by a large boulder, shielding themselves from the icy winds that came from the north, and built an oven of turf and flat rocks to cook the meat of the goat they had slain.

After some time, Loki checked the meat and found that it was ice cold. The fire was burning hot, though, so he did not understand why their dinner would not cook. He put more wood in the oven to make the fire even hotter.

Some time went by, and Loki checked the food once more, but it was still ice cold. In fact, it seemed as if the meat had gotten even colder. The three gods were very befuddled by this. Loki added even *more* wood to the fire, making it so hot that it was sure to char parts of the goat. This time he also blew so hard at the fire that the flames licked the sides of the meat.

Loki tried feeling the meat once again, but it was still cold to the touch! Then he cursed loudly and asked aloud what was wrong.

"I am responsible for keeping the meat from cooking!" boomed a voice from above. The three gods looked up and saw a huge eagle sitting on the top of the boulder. The eagle flapped his wings—it seemed that they filled the whole sky and covered up the sun.

"Who are you?" Odin asked.

The eagle answered him, "I am Thjazi and I live in this valley. It is my herd of goats that you have stolen from! If you wish to eat, you will have to share with your host!"

Odin agreed to these terms and invited the eagle to join them. Soon after, the meat was cooked, hot and crisp. But when they took the goat out of the oven, the eagle Thjazi swooped down and snatched the meat away, leaving only the skin and bones.

Loki was furious. He grabbed his walking stick and began to beat at the eagle. The eagle leapt back, clamped its claws on the stick, then bashed its mighty wings and flew high into the sky with Loki dangling below. Loki screamed and clung to the stick, terrified of falling. His arms and shoulders began to hurt from hanging on to the stick so tight.

They flew over mountains and forests, and Loki shrieked and squirmed as his feet hit the treetops. "Please let me down!" Loki cried. "What can I do to save myself? I will do anything!"

"Anything?" the eagle asked.

"Anything!" Loki said.

"Then you must bring me Idun, the goddess of eternal renewal, the goddess of youth. That is my demand."

Loki agreed to this, so the eagle put him safely back down on the ground, where he rejoined Odin and Honir.

The three gods went back to Asgard where Loki found Idun picking apples in the garden. Loki went over to her and said, "You know, there's a grove outside the walls of Asgard where I have seen the most beautiful tree with the biggest apples on it. Why don't you come with me and compare the apples you have there with the ones on that tree?"

Idun did not suspect a thing, and she agreed to follow Loki out of Asgard to a grove called Barri. Loki told no one where he was taking her. As soon as they entered the clearing, a dark shadow fell over the grove, and Thjazi flew down, swiped Idun off her feet, and carried her off to his home in Thrymheim.

When Idun disappeared, all the gods fell under a curious spell and began to age rapidly. Their hair turned gray, their skin wrinkled, and their voices became frail. Odin called a council, and they all sat down by the world tree, Yggdrasill, to try to determine where Idun had disappeared to. Heimdall said that he had last seen her with Loki leaving Asgard's enclosures.

Thor, despite how elderly he had grown, still had a little strength in him, so he grabbed Loki and stuck holes in his heels, put a rope through the holes, and strung Loki up in a tree. Thor lit a fire under Loki's head and let him cook for some time before Loki screamed in terror and told the gods the truth about Idun's whereabouts. The gods told Loki that if he wanted to keep his life, he would have to go to Thrymheim to retrieve Idun and bring her back to Asgard.

Loki changed his shape to a falcon and was quickly on his way. He flew north to the far lands in Jotunheim, and there he found Thrymheim, Thjazi's home. When he arrived, Thjazi was out fishing on the sea, and Idun was alone in the house. She sat at a loom, weaving a beautiful tapestry. Loki landed on the windowsill and told her to come with him to Asgard. When she came to the window, Loki sang *galdr, song*-magic, which turned her into a little nut so that he could carry her in his claws, and they were quickly on their way.

But Thjazi saw the falcon flying and recognized the little nut in its claws as Idun. He bashed his wings and raised a storm as he took off. He was coming after them! All the world's seas were in an uproar, and the sky turned dark gray.

Loki the falcon flew in haste, through the deep valleys, over jagged rocks, between birch and pine trees, but Thjazi the eagle was right on his heels. Then they came within sight of Asgard's wall, and Loki said to Idun, "Soon we'll be there! The eagle can't catch us once we cross to Asgard!"

Heimdall stood on the tallest cliff on his mountain, Himinbjorg, and watched the falcon's flight and the eagle's chase. He called out to the gods down below, "I see a falcon with a nut in his claws and an eagle in pursuit!"

The gods knew that this was Loki and Thjazi, so they brought a great heap of wood shavings to the wall and lit a huge bonfire. The falcon swooped in over the wall and let himself drop down just before the bonfire, but the eagle couldn't stop quickly enough, for he was too big and too fast. Just as the eagle's claws snapped at Loki, the eagle fell into the fire and burst into flames.

With Idun's return, the gods regained their strength and youthful appearance and held a large feast to celebrate. Everyone was invited, large and small, dwarfs and elves. All of Asgard was cheerful that day. But the happy days would soon come to an end because Thjazi's daughter was bound to seek revenge.

SKADI'S
MARRIAGE TO NJORD

hjazi's daughter, Skadi—also called Ondurdis—was sitting in her halls in Thrymheim when she heard the news of her father's death. A young shepherd ran in from the pastures and told her that he had learned how the gods had burned the great eagle—Skadi's father!

The warrior daughter of Thjazi did not take this loss well. She was drinking from a golden cup when she heard this, but she clutched it so hard that the gold turned into liquid. Then she went to her room and put on her helmet and armor and took up her weapons of war.

Skadi put on her skis and pushed hard, propelling herself down the snowy mountains. Ice and wind did not stop her, and when she finally came to Asgard's wall, her braids were frozen icicles. She called out with a mighty battle cry, "I will have revenge for the death of my father!"

The gods were not at all happy to see her there. They gathered in council to decide what to do. Tyr the Brave came up with a plan: "Why don't we offer her to pick from among the unwed gods a fine husband?

This should appease her!" The gods all agreed on this. Tyr went outside the wall to barter with Skadi.

Skadi calmed herself and said, "Fine, I will take a husband from among you. The one I want is Balder because he is best and brightest and most beautiful."

"It will not work that way," Tyr answered. "You must pick one based on seeing only their feet." And this was the agreement.

All the gods stood behind a long linen so that Skadi could only see their bare feet. She walked along the line, wondering to herself which pair of feet belonged to Balder. Then she saw a pair of feet so smooth and pretty that she thought they must be Balder's. Skadi declared, "I choose this man! There can be nothing ugly about Balder." But she was mistaken. It was not Balder, but Njord of Noatun, the castle at the coast. Njord would be Skadi's husband. Skadi was not happy about this, but it was the agreement, so she accepted it.

It was also part of the agreement that before Skadi left Asgard, one of the gods had to make her laugh. This was a difficult task because her heart was broken from the loss of her father, but Loki had come up with a plan. He took a cord and tied one end of it to a goat's beard and the other end to his own. Loki and the goat drew back and forth and they both squealed. At the end, Loki, red all over his face, fell into Skadi's lap, and the goat ran off, rather unhappy with it all. Loki looked into Skadi's eyes, and she burst out into a deep, roaring laughter.

The gods did one last thing to make her happy and give her father a good memory: Thor took Thjazi's eyes and threw them into the sky. Up there on heaven's vault, Thjazi's eyes became two bright shining stars that still stand today in memory of the great eagle.

Skadi and Njord had a beautiful wedding ceremony and, even though Skadi had hoped to marry Balder, she fell deeply in love with Njord of Noatun. They went to live in Thrymheim, Thjazi's place in the mountains, but Njord woke up every night to the noise of howling wolves and the hard winds. One day he said, "I hate mountains, and I hate the howling of the wolves. But I love the singing swans! Why do I stay here as a peasant in the mountains when I can be on the sea, where the waves crash and the whales play? I long for my ship's prow to plough the waves and my sword to play in open battle—the life of a Viking—that brings honor and fame to my family's name!"

Skadi looked at her husband and felt sad for him. She told him that they could move to Noatun, his castle by the coast, and then he would not feel so homesick. So, they packed up and left and went to the sea.

They stayed at the sea for a while, but then, one night, Skadi woke up and said, "I can't sleep in my bed at sea! The birds are screaming, and the seagulls wake me too early every morning! The waves crash on the land with a roar, and I hate their splashing and foaming! I long for the deep, dark woods and snowcapped mountains!"

After some talk, they decided that Njord would stay in Noatun and Skadi would go back to live in Thrymheim. There, the bright bride of the gods ruled her father's old lands in the deep forests and snow-capped mountains. She hunted on skis, ran with howling wolves, and flew with the hawks.

Njord, meanwhile, lived in Noatun by the sea. He fished every day and sailed the waves in his Viking ship with flocks of seagulls following close behind. His ship, made by the dwarfs that made Thor's hammer, was such a special creation that it could be folded into a little leaf, which Njord could then carry in his pocket. Njord's love for Skadi was still strong and her love for him remained unchanged, so once every ninth night, they met in the sacred grove called Barri. Together, they had a daughter named Ran.

One day, when Ran was walking along the shore near her father's house, she met a man named Agir. He was tall and handsome and came from the Jotnar. They decided to meet again, and Ran said to Agir, "Next time you come, be neither dressed nor undressed, neither hungry nor full, neither alone nor with anybody." This was her test for him. The next time they met, Agir stood there on the beach, wrapped in a fishing net, chewing on some seaweed, with a seal at his side. Ran couldn't stop laughing. They fell deeply in love and decided to get married. Agir's great hall, Gymisgard, was deep below the waves of the sea. It was made of gold and crystal, and the mermen and mermaids lived with him down there. Sometimes they came up to land in the shape of seals. One must be nice to them, as they ensure safe travel on the ocean.

Agir invited all the mermaids and mermen to a great feast to celebrate his wedding, and Ran went to live with Agir in the deep sea. She caught the unfortunate sailors who drowned with her net and invited them to stay with her and Agir in their palace. Ran and Agir had nine daughters: Himingleva, Dufa, Blodughadda, Hefring, Unn, Hronn, Bylgia, Bara, and Kolga. They appeared as waves, whales, seals, seaweed, fish, or any other kind of animal that lived in the sea. Their job was to help Ran care for sailors and ensure safe passage for them. Often, all they needed in return is bread with salt on it, a pair of pants, or a mitten. Ran's daughters gave these things to the sailors down there because sometimes it can get very cold at the bottom of the ocean.

Geirrod,
the King in Jotunheim's Caves

urvandil was a very strong young warrior in the land of Frost-Sweden who was skilled in many things. He was a good craftsman, a great hunter, and an excellent sailor and fisherman. One day, he was out hunting and came across a lonely house in the woods. Outside the house stood a beautiful woman named Gjalp. She spoke to him with familiarity. She knew his name and everything about him, and the words she spoke became a spell that captivated Aurvandil. He couldn't resist her magic eyes and her bright red lips that spoke ensnaring words. At her beckoning, he went with her, through the door to her house. But suddenly, the house was gone! It was replaced by a giant boulder. Gjalp had tricked Aurvandil to follow her into the underworld kingdom, ruled by her evil father, the Jotun Geirrod.

When Aurvandil didn't return home that evening, his mother, Groa, began to wonder where he was. She sent out birds to find him: king-fishers to look over the lakes and rivers, jackdaws to look for him in the woods, starlings to look for him in the heaths, fulmars to look for him on the ocean, and warblers to look for him on the taiga. But he was nowhere to be found.

Saddened by the loss of her son, Groa went to Thrudheim to find Thor and tell him what had happened. Sif said to her husband Thor that she did not think that Aurvandil had disappeared without some kind of mischief and that Thor should seek out Geirrod. "Since he rules the underworld kingdom in Jotunheim," Sif said, "he is likely to know something about this."

Groa said, "Here, take my iron rod on your journey. It may come in handy if you are in distress. Geirrod is not a pleasant Jotun!" Soon, Thor was on his way across Middle Earth with his servant Thjalfi at his side.

They passed easily through the deep fir woods and crossed the open taiga, but then they came to a large river called Vimur. The currents were strong and kept getting stronger. Thor used Groa's iron rod to keep his balance, while Thjalfi held on tight to Thor's belt. When they were in the middle of the river, the current was so strong that Thor was almost swept away. Thor grabbed Thjalfi and threw him to safety on the far bank. Then he noticed that there was someone far up along the river who was making the current so violent—it was the Jotun Gjalp!

Thor picked up a large rock from the bottom of the river and threw it at Gjalp, hitting her right in the head. He cried out, "Stay calm, river, don't rise! I want to wade across. If you rise, my strength will rise just as much, as high as heaven's vault." Then Thjalfi reached out to Thor with a branch of a rowan tree, saving him from being swept away in the water. That is why the rowan tree is called Thor's Salvation.

Thor and Thjalfi forged ahead, following the river upstream. Far up in the mountains, they came to a cave from where the river Vimur rushed out. There was just enough space for them to squeeze through next to the water, and they walked for a long time through the cave, until finally they came to a great hall. Everything inside was made of rocks: the seats, tables, glasses, plates, all of it. They sat down to rest for a while, since their journey had been so long.

As Thor and Thjalfi were sitting on a bench, they felt it moving. Suddenly, the ground rushed toward the ceiling. They were going to be crushed against the rock roof! Just in time, Thor took out Groa's iron rod and pushed it so hard against the ceiling that the bench broke. Then, they heard a great scream and realized that Greip, Gjalp's sister, had made herself into the stone bench. She had been trying to crush them to death, but now, her back was broken.

Free from the stone bench, Thor and Thjalfi walked down the hall and came across a huge fireplace that held burning rocks. It was dark at the end of the hall, but then a pair of eyes as large and bright as two moons appeared in the darkness. Then a mouth appeared, which was so big that it stretched from one end of the cave to the other. It began speaking, "I am Geirrod. Who is this that enters my hall? Tell me your name!"

Thor picked up one of the molten rocks with his iron gloves and threw it at the giant mouth. They heard a great scream, and Thor rushed forward with Groa's iron rod and thrust it at Geirrod, killing the Jotun. With a loud crack, the stone walls around them began to shake. The roof came tumbling down and rocks fell everywhere. Thjalfi spread his eagle wings, and he and Thor flew out just as the cave crumbled. Rocks and stone, dust and smoke were everywhere, and the river Vimur rushed out of the cave.

Safely outside, Thor looked around until he spotted poor Aurvandil lying in the river, cut into seven pieces. Thor used Groa's iron rod to collect Aurvandil's pieces and place them in a basket to carry back home with him. Thor and Thjalfi traveled a long time, over the river Vimur, across the open taiga, and through the deep fir woods.

When they finally came to Groa's house, Thor told Groa everything that had happened and how they had found Aurvandil in seven pieces. When Thor showed her the basket that held the many pieces of Aurvandil, Groa was happy that they had brought her son back to her. She chanted this *galdr* song over him:

"Once, the Disir sat here, then they sat there, then they sat here. Some fastened bonds, fastened fate, spun threads for all. Sol's sister spun them, so did Fulla's sister and Frigg herself, as well as she could. Like bone-sprain, so blood-sprain, so joint-sprain. Bone to bone, blood to blood, joint to joint. So, may they be glued!"

With that song, Groa put Aurvandil back together. His body rejoined in all the right places, and he woke up from a deep slumber. But there was one piece that couldn't be glued back to his body. During the journey back, one of Aurvandil's toes had frozen, which meant that Groa's *galdr* didn't work on it. Thor took the toe and threw it into the sky, and it became the star that the Vikings called Aurvandil's Toe.

HRUNGNIR
INVADES ASGARD

ne day, Odin rode his eight-legged horse, Sleipnir, deep into Jotunheim, the land of the Jotnar. As he was riding through the mountains there, Odin came to a deep gorge with a bridge to cross. But once he arrived at the bridge, he noticed a huge boulder. The boulder began to move, and before Odin knew it, a giant man made entirely of rock stood up in front of him. The man made of rock said, "Who are you and what are you doing here?"

Odin answered, "I am Odin, ruler of the gods! I want to cross the bridge. Who are you?"

The giant replied, "I am Hrungnir, the god of rocks! My head is made of stone and so is my heart. The only way you will cross this bridge is as a corpse."

Odin thought to himself for a moment, and then he said, "What if we race? My horse Sleipnir is the strongest and fastest of all horses in the world."

Hrungnir answered, "Ha! My horse Gullfaxi is much faster! I'll race you, and when I win, I'll have your head!"

Odin took off as fast as Sleipnir could run. Hrungnir followed right after. The two galloped so hard that they soon reached Asgard. Hrungnir was in such a rage and fury that he did not realize how far they had traveled, and he found himself rushing through the gates of Valhall itself. Inside the gates, Hrungnir got off his horse and walked through the hall looking for Odin, who had indeed outraced him. There he saw Odin sitting on the throne.

Odin said, "A guest has entered! Feed him well and bring him much to drink." The cup that Thor usually drank from was brought out, and mead was poured into it.

Hrungnir began drinking, and after some time, he got very drunk and began talking loudly and angrily. He said, "I am going to take Valhall to Jotunheim! I'm going to bury Asgard deep under the earth in a pile of rocks! And I'm going to kill all you gods! But I will take the beautiful goddesses Freya and Sif home with me."

Odin replied, "The more a man drinks, the less he knows! You shouldn't clutch your cup, but drink in moderation, and spare your speech or shut up entirely. No one was ever blamed for going to bed early."

Hrungnir got up from his seat in such a rush that he knocked over the table with his knees. He grabbed his weapon, the mighty flint stone, and was just about to throw it at Odin, but then there was a loud roar of thunder. A lightning bolt struck down in the middle of the hall, and when the dust cleared, Thor was standing in front of Hrungnir. Thor's hammer, Mjollnir, was raised and he was ready to throw it straight at the drunken Jotun's head.

Hrungnir sobered up at the sight of Thor and pleaded for his life. "Mighty Thor, you wouldn't kill a man in the sanctuary of the gods'

home! It is the custom of the gods to offer peace and safety to anyone who enters their halls. I was invited here by Odin himself!"

Thor acknowledged that this was true and said, "Instead, I will meet you in a duel. You can choose the site." It was decided that they would meet at a place in the mountains called Grjotun, the Rock Yard. Each of them could bring a helper to the duel, and they would fight with their own weapons. After they had agreed on the terms of the duel, Hrungnir quickly got back on his horse and galloped away from Asgard.

When Hrungnir arrived home in Jotunheim, he gathered all the other Jotnar to discuss the duel. Much was at stake for the Jotnar, and they did not think it would be good fortune for them if Thor killed Hrungnir, so they decided to use all the magic they knew to create a powerful helper for Hrungnir in the duel. A Jotun named Grid said that she had overheard Odin's *galdr* (song-magic) and from that she had learned how to make a man from clay. So, the Jotnar created the giant Mokkurkalfi. He was nine leagues tall and three leagues wide over the chest. But because Grid did not know the magic *galdr* song well enough, the Jotnar couldn't make a heart for Mokkurkalfi. Instead, they used the tiny heart of a mole.

On the day of the duel, Hrungnir and Mokkurkalfi were waiting at Grjotun in the early morning mist. Hrungnir had his flint stone with him as well as a giant stone shield. Mokkurkalfi did not bring along a weapon, thinking his massive size would serve him well in the duel.

For his own helper in the duel, Thor had chosen Thjalfi, the fastest runner in the world. Thjalfi set out ahead of Thor to Grjotun. When he came to the field, he saw Hrungnir and Mokkurkalfi and went over to them. Thjalfi went up to Hrungnir and said, "You're a fool! You're holding your shield as if Thor is going to attack you from the front, but most often, the Thunder God travels below ground, and that is how he'll attack you." Hrungnir asked Thjalfi what he should do. Thjalfi said, "You should put your shield under your feet and stand on it so that Thor will hit that when he comes up from his travels on the roads of Hel."

Hrungnir did what Thjalfi told him to, but as soon as he stepped on his shield, a black cloud appeared in the blue sky, and Thor came flying down in a burst of thunder and lightning. Without wasting a moment, Thor threw his hammer, Mjollnir, straight at Hrungnir. When Hrungnir saw this, he threw his flint rock back at Thor. Mjollnir darted through the air and hit the flint rock so hard that it shattered into billions of pieces, and then it struck Hrungnir right in the head. It is said that all the stones that can be used to sharpen iron come from that flint rock that Mjollnir shattered that day. Hrungnir, in turn, lost his head.

When Mokkurkalfi saw this, he wet himself in fear. Thjalfi used his speed and flight to attack Mokkurkalfi, and the giant clay man quickly fell with little glory. When the duel was over and the dust had settled, all the gods gathered at Grjotun. But there was one god who was not standing: Thor. When Hrungnir had fallen, his leg had landed on top of Thor, and the stone man was too big to push off. That is when Thor's son, Magni, went to Thor and lifted Hrungnir's leg to free his father. Thor hugged Magni and said that he would grow up to be a strong warrior. Then he took Hrungnir's horse Gullfaxi and gave it to Magni as a gift.

A curious thing had happened in the battle between Thor and Hrungnir. One of the pieces of flint that came from Hrungnir's weapon had shot straight into Thor's forehead and gotten stuck. It was lodged so deeply in Thor's head that no one could get it out. That is why you should never throw a stone used to sharpen iron across a floor: It is said that if you do, the stone in Thor's forehead moves and gives him a terrible headache that provokes him to send down thunder and lightning.

ODIN
AND THE MEAD OF POETRY

When the world's first war ended, all the gods spat into a great cauldron as a way to confirm their intentions of peace. After the other gods had gone away, Loki went up to the cauldron and sang a *galdr* song over it. Suddenly, the spittle inside the cauldron came to life, and Loki created a man named Kvasir from it. Kvasir immediately began traveling and went to many different places and met many different peoples throughout the world. He visited the seas, the mountains, the woods, the taiga, the lakes, the marshes, the plains, and everywhere else, and he often found interesting people to talk to.

Kvasir also visited the gods and the elves, and, one day, he found himself with the dwarfs in their land of Nidavellir. Two dwarfs, Fjalar and Galar, invited him into their home. When Kvasir sat down and shared his stories of travel, Fjalar grew incredibly envious and enraged. Without warning, Fjalar swiftly stuck his knife in Kvasir and bled him dry. He and Galar then poured Kvasir's blood in a large pot called

Odrerir and mixed it with honey. They let the mixture stand for some time, and then they sang *galdr* songs over it. In this manner, they made mead, and the mead became magical—so magical that anyone who drank from it would receive the gift of poetry and would be able to compose great poems.

Soon after this happened, a Jotun named Gilling came to visit the dwarfs. Fjalar, Galar, and Gilling decided to go sailing, but their trip took an unfortunate turn and the boat capsized, drowning Gilling. When the dwarfs came back to shore, they told Gilling's wife of his fate, and she was so sad that she couldn't stop crying. Finally, Fjalar had enough of her tears and told Gilling's wife to go stand in the doorway of their rock house so that she could see the ocean and feel soothed. Fjalar, however, had a more sinister plan. He quietly snuck up on the roof and threw a boulder down on her head as she mourned so that she died, too.

When Gilling's brother, Suttung, heard about the death of his brother and sister-in-law, he was very angry. He went to the dwarfs and brought them out on the sea in their little boat. Then he pushed them out of the boat, meaning for them to drown. As they were splashing around in the water, struggling to stay afloat, Fjalar said to Suttung, "You can have our precious mead in turn for letting us live!" Suttung decided that this was a good trade-off, so he accepted the deal. He brought the mead home with him to the mountain Hnitbjorg where he lived, placed the mead deep within the mountain, and told his daughter Gunlod to watch over it.

Word of this magical mead reached Odin, who was very interested in it and wanted to bring it back home to Asgard. Odin dressed up as a traveler and took off for Jotunheim. He walked for a very long time through the woods, the mountains, the taiga, the meadows, over the plains, along the shores, and across many rivers.

When he got to the fields around the home of Baugi, Suttung's brother, he found nine dwarfs working. They were harvesting, but their scythes were very dull, and it took them a long time to cut the hay. Odin walked up to them and introduced himself as Bolverk, the name he had taken to disguise himself. Then he said, "I can see that your scythes are dull. Would you like me to show you how to make them sharper?" They all eagerly said "yes," and he then used a stone to sharpen their scythes. After the dwarfs saw how easily the scythes cut the grass, they all wanted to buy the stone from Bolverk, but he threw it into the air. The dwarfs scrambled to catch it, and then they began to fight over it, eventually killing each other over the stone.

When Baugi saw that all the dwarfs were dead in the field, he came out and shouted, "What has happened? How am I supposed to harvest for winter when all my workers are dead?" Odin, disguised as Bolverk, answered that he would happily do the work of the nine dwarfs if Baugi, in turn, would help him get a drink of the precious magical mead of poetry that his brother Suttung was keeping in the mountain. Baugi agreed to this, and soon thereafter all his hay was harvested long before winter had even begun.

Baugi and Bolverk then went to Suttung and asked for the magical mead, but Suttung did not want to share any of it. Bolverk said to Baugi that he still owed him since he had done all that hard work for him. Baugi had promised to help Bolverk, so he agreed to go up on the mountain with him and find a way inside it. Baugi started drilling into the mountain while Bolverk kept watch.

After Baugi had been drilling for a while, Bolverk blew into the hole to see how far he had gotten. Many rocks fell out, but Bolverk saw that the hole was still very small. He made Baugi drill some more, and when there was finally a hole deep enough into the mountain, Bolverk turned himself into a snake and slipped into the hole.

As soon as he was inside the mountain, Bolverk found Suttung's daughter, Gunlod, sleeping in a big, comfortable bed. He woke her up and made her an offer: He, Bolverk, would stay with her for nine nights in exchange for a sip of the mead. She agreed.

After nine nights had gone by, Bolverk leapt up and drank not just one sip but *all* the mead in one gulp. Then he turned into an eagle and used all his might to burst out of the mountain as quickly as he could. He flew down over the fields and out over the plains, heading straight for Asgard.

Suttung saw Bolverk take off and quickly turned his arms into wings and his legs into a feathery tail. He made a storm with his wings when he took flight. The two eagles flew hard and fast through the world. They flew over the mountains and glaciers, over sea and ice, over rivers and lakes and marshes, through the woods and over the taiga.

Eventually, they came to Asgard. Heimdall, the watchman of the gods, saw the two eagles coming, and he recognized the faster eagle as Odin. He called out to the gods to bring a big cauldron. When they had placed the cauldron below the gates of Asgard, Odin flew right over the wall and dipped down. He then threw up most of the mead that he had carried in his belly all this time, and it landed in the cauldron. But the last bit of mead that he had in him, he spit out backward, right into Suttung's face. The giant eagle was blinded by the mead and flew straight into the wall, cracking his skull on the hard rocks.

This is how Odin brought the mead of poetry to the gods. It is said that when you drink from it, you become wise and creative. In the old days, when the Vikings had court poets, these poets would drink from that mead, and that is how they made their poetry about kings, heroes, gods, and battles. But the bad poets, it is said, were the ones that drank from the part of the mead that Odin sent out backward in Suttung's face.

JORMUNGAND,
THE GREAT SEA SERPENT

O n one of his journeys when he was young, Thor walked across the world to the Great Sea in the North, where the frost-Jotun Hymir lived on his farm. Hymir was out fishing when Thor arrived, so the lady of the household showed him in and told him to take a seat behind one of the great pillars in Hymir's hall.

Not long after Thor sat down, Hymir came through the door. Icicles dangled from his frozen beard, and he had a mean look in his eyes. He was not happy to see Thor in his home. He stared directly at the pillar in front of Thor, and the wood shattered from his glare. Just as Hymir reached for his fishing hook to fight, Thor said, "Oh, great Hymir, remember the ancient laws! A guest has entered. The far-traveled needs a warm fire when they are cold to their knees, water to drink, and food in their belly."

At that, Hymir had six fat salmon brought out, fresh and steaming hot. Thor ate all six, but he was still hungry. Then Hymir brought out three roasted oxen. Thor gobbled them down along with a big barrel of ale. Hymir was quite amazed and said, "With the way you eat, boy, we have to go fishing tomorrow! Sleep now, and tomorrow we will take my boat, but you will have to supply your own bait."

In the morning, Thor woke up as the icy wind from the sea rushed through the door. Hymir was already awake and collecting his fishing gear. When Thor asked where he could find bait, Hymir just shrugged. Thor went to the stables and saw Hymir's favorite giant ox. He grabbed the ox by the horns and ripped off its head. Then he took a ship's anchor that was hanging on the wall, pierced it through the ox's head, and said, "Now I'm ready to go fishing!"

Hymir looked at what Thor had done to his favorite ox and said, "You have done me no favor, boy. Let's see how well you fare on the icy waves. Little ones like you don't tend to take well to the piercing ice drops that the monster Jormungand spews over fishermen in the northern seas."

Hymir jumped into the boat and told Thor to push it out. The keel was stuck in the sand, but Thor pressed against it with all his strength, and the boat rushed into the waves so fast that sparks flew from where it hit the rocks. Once the boat was out to sea, Thor took the oars and started rowing. Soon, Hymir said, "This is where I usually catch flat fish. Let us cast anchor and begin fishing." But Thor said no and rowed farther out.

A little later Hymir said, "This is where I usually catch cod. Let's stay here. The waves get much bigger further out." Thor shook his head and jerked so hard at the oars that the boat broke the waves with a mighty splash.

After some time had passed, Hymir said that they were now so far out that he feared Jormungand, the monstrous sea serpent, would be a danger to them. Thor looked at Hymir with a spark in his eyes and said, "Good!" Then he threw the ox head on the anchor overboard with such force that the chain carved a deep groove in the side of the boat.

The wind was howling, the waves were crashing on the sides of the boat, and icy rain was coming down hard on the two fishermen. Hymir caught two whales before he turned around to see what Thor had caught. When he saw that Thor's bucket was still empty, Hymir laughed so loud that it echoed in the heaven's vault. But Thor had laid his line with cunning and he had good patience, so he waited a little longer. Just as Hymir turned around a second time to tell him to row back, Thor felt his line jerk. One slight jerk, then another. Suddenly, something tugged at the line so hard that Thor fell forward and his knuckles smashed against the boat.

Thor pulled on the line. He pulled so hard that the skin on his knuckles broke. The creature down below pulled even harder. Hymir felt the boat tipping from the weight of creature's pull, and he turned around, his face as pale as ash, and screamed, "You have hooked Jormungand, you crazy boy!"

Thor turned his head and looked at him with piercing eyes and a menacing grin. In the distance behind him, Hymir could see the shape of the mighty serpent coming up through the waves. Thor raised himself from his seat, stood up in the boat, and pulled harder on the line. He pulled so hard that a loud *crack* was heard all across the northern seas and his feet went through the bottom of the boat.

Thor summoned all his god strength and power, and he grew much taller than he was before. His feet were on the bottom of the ocean, the waves were crashing around his waist, and his head with its high, fire-red hair was above the clouds. He pulled so hard that he lifted Jormungand out of the waves and drew the serpent's head so close that they were now staring each other straight in the eyes. Thor ground his teeth, and his eyes shot lightning. Jormungand spewed icy saltwater back at Thor.

Hymir, terrified of the giant sea serpent, panicked and drew his fishing knife. He hacked at the frozen chain that had drawn Jormungand up from the depths of the ocean and split it in two. The serpent fell back in the sea with a splash that could be heard across the world. Thor threw his hammer, Mjollnir, into the depth of the waves where it darted to the bottom and gave a loud crash that resonated across the ocean floor.

Some say that Thor killed the serpent that day, while others believe that it still lives out there in the depths of the Great Sea. Either way, Thor was not pleased with Hymir for freeing his catch. He stared that old man in the eyes, flames shooting from his hair and beard, and said with a voice that echoed throughout the depths of the universe, "I am Odin's son, Fire-rider! Warden of the temples! Protector of humanity!" Then he swung his fist and struck Hymir so hard on his cheek that the ogre plunged into the ocean and sank to the bottom with his feet in the air.

Thor threw the two whales on his shoulders and waded ashore. It is said that when Thor reached land again, he was so big and his heavy feet pressed down with such force that his footprints became the inlets that can still be seen up on Nastrond, in the cold North, at the edge of the world. Thor gave one whale to Hymir's widow and walked home to Asgard with the other one over his shoulder. And that is the story of how Thor fought Jormungand, the Great Serpent, the creature that encircles the entire earth.

FENRIR,
THE VENGEFUL WOLF

nce, Loki went in the shape of a hawk to explore Jotunheim. He flew far and wide, crossing great distances. When he came to a forest called Jarnvid, he decided that he needed a break, so he landed in the top of a great pine tree.

As he was sitting there, he could see a lake not far from him and, at the shore of that lake, a little house. Loki wanted to know who lived in that house, so he flew over to it, dropped down through the chimney hole in the roof, and perched on one of the crossbeams near the ceiling.

It was odd. Loki could hear people talking inside the house, but he didn't see anyone. He heard an old man talking with a young woman, and he understood from their conversation that it was an aging father and his daughter. He moved closer to where the sound came from, unaware that he accidentally kicked some dust off the beam he was sitting on. As the dust fell down, the old man became aware that there was someone in the house. He said, "Listen, daughter, do you hear anything? I don't think we're alone in the house."

The daughter replied, "I hear nothing, father. Why do you think that?"

He said, "I saw dust falling from the crossbeam over there."

As Loki heard him say that, he flew up toward the hole in the ceiling in order to escape. But when he reached it, he couldn't fly through. He could see the sky, but he could not pass! After trying several times, Loki's wings got tired, and he had to sit down on the crossbeam again.

Suddenly, he saw the old man coming toward him. He recognized that both the old man and the young woman were Huldur, the kind of elves that look like people but have tails. Loki tried to escape again, but this time, he couldn't even lift his feet from the crossbeam, and he realized that the old man was using magic to keep him in the house.

The old man crawled up to the beam and grabbed the hawk. When he looked into the hawk's eyes and saw that there was a person in there, he said, "Who are you and why are you sneaking around in our house?"

Loki said, "I'm Loki. I wasn't doing anything! I was just curious!"

The old man said, "Curiosity killed the cat! We don't take kindly to strangers sneaking into our house this way. You're in a Huldur-rock now! This is where the Huldur-trolls live, and chances are you'll never escape." He used his magic to force Loki out of his hawk shape, and then he chained Loki to a rock by the fireplace.

For some time, Loki was the Huldur's captive. The old man treated him like a dog and fed him scraps from the table. But when the old man wasn't home, Loki spent his time talking with the daughter, Angerboda. When the old man was out fishing on the lake, Loki pleaded with Angerboda to let him go, saying that the gods in Asgard were wondering where he was and that they were probably looking for him by now. He promised that he would bring her with him, if she let him go. Angerboda, who had fallen in love with Loki and wanted to leave with him, obliged and unlocked the chains. As soon as she did,

Loki turned into a hawk and flew out of the chimney hole in the roof, leaving her behind.

Angerboda was greatly saddened by Loki's lie and his disappearance. She wept for nine months. At the end of the nine months, she gave birth to a child and called him Fenrir. After just three days, Fenrir was nearly fully grown. He was no ordinary boy. He had a tail like his mother, but he also had a snout, fur, and the ears of a wolf. Soon, he was a massive wolf that just kept growing and growing.

Back in Asgard, Loki was carefree and jolly, not giving a single thought to what had happened with the Huldra Angerboda. But then, one day, Loki was sitting under a tree when two sparrows flew up and rested on a branch above him. One of the sparrows said to the other, "Have you heard about the wolf called Fenrir? It is said that he is looking for his father, Loki, and it seems he is headed this way to Asgard."

When Loki heard this, he jumped up and rushed to Himinbjorg, where the watcher god Heimdall lives. He asked Heimdall to see if he could spot a wolf that was heading to Asgard. Heimdall looked out over the worlds and said, "Yes, I see a huge, monstrous wolf walking through the deep, dark woods in the distance. And he is coming this way!" Loki rushed to Odin and told him what had happened in the Huldur-rock and that the wolf was coming to Asgard. Odin said, "This is your spawn! You'll have to welcome him and treat him as your son." And that was the end of it.

When Fenrir arrived at Asgard, he was so big that none of the gods felt safe around him. Only Tyr the Brave would spend time with the wolf and feed him. Odin, in particular, was nervous around Fenrir because the wolf had arrived shortly after Hel told Odin that he would fall before a wolf at Ragnarok. Would Fenrir be the prophesied wolf to end Odin's life?

Odin journeyed to Hel once again. In Hel's halls, Odin asked, "What will be the end of Odin?"

Hel said, "The Father of Men will be swallowed by the wolf, but Vidar the Silent will avenge this and rip open its cold jaws in the midst of battle." When Odin learned this, he knew that the wolf Hel spoke of must be Fenrir. He went back to Asgard and devised a plan: He would trick Fenrir into letting himself be tied up so he could not be a threat.

Odin went to the dwarfs Brokk and Eitri and told them to make a chain, which they called Leyding. Odin then took Leyding to Fenrir and said, "Wolf! Let me see how strong you are! Try your strength with this chain around your neck." Fenrir didn't think much of it and let himself be chained by Leyding. When he shook his head, the chain immediately broke.

Odin went back to the dwarfs and asked them to make a chain that was twice as strong. They made the chain called Dromi, and Odin went back to Fenrir. "Here, see if you can break *this* chain!" Fenrir thought to himself that it was a little risky but that he probably could break this chain, too. Odin laid the chain around Fenrir's neck, and as soon as the wolf scratched himself with his hind leg, Dromi broke.

Odin went back to the dwarfs in Nidavellir and said, "Make me a new chain! Here are the things you must use: the sound of a cat's paws, the roots of a mountain, the sinews of a bear, breath from a fish, the spittle from a bird, and the howling from the wolves at night." Soon after, the dwarfs gave Odin a chain called Gleipnir. By this time, though, Fenrir was on to Odin and didn't trust him one bit. Odin told Tyr that the next time he was going to feed Fenrir, he must talk the wolf into letting himself be chained by Gleipnir.

The next day, Tyr took the chain and walked down to the lake Amsvartnir, where Fenrir roamed. There, he met the wolf and said, "Fenrir, will you try your strength against this chain?" Fenrir said, "It seems like a thin rope, but I have no reason to trust the gods, so if you want to put that around my neck, you must put your hand in my mouth first." Tyr agreed to this and put his hand in Fenrir's mouth. Then, with his other hand, he took Gleipnir and locked it around Fenrir's neck. The wolf stretched and tore at the chain, but nothing helped. He was stuck.

Angered that he had been tricked, the wolf clamped his jaws down over Tyr's hand, biting it off at the wrist. Tyr used his sword to pry open the wolf's mouth and propped Fenrir's jaws up by placing the point of the sword in his upper gums and the hilt in his bottom gums. Then Tyr took a rock, wrapped Gleipnir around it, and thrust it into the ground. That is how Fenrir was caught. Fenrir lies there with his jaws propped open, howling horribly. It is said that the saliva that runs from his mouth is the source of the river Gjoll. Fenrir will be tied there until Ragnarok, and Tyr will forever be known as the one-handed god.

THE SONG OF THE
VALKYRIES

When warriors went to battle, the female war spirits called Valkyries followed behind them, and when warriors died, the Valkyries picked them up and brought them to Odin's and Freya's halls. It is said that the Valkyries carried armor, helmets, weapons, and shields.

There were many kinds of Valkyries. Some followed the warriors to the battlefield, some protected families, and others were spirits that lived among us. The Valkyries could appear as birds, wolves, foxes, cats, and seals. No one knew all the names of the Valkyries, but some of them were called Hrist, Mist, Skegold, Skogul, Hild, Thrud, Hlokk, Herfjotur, Goll, Geirondul, Randgrid, Radgrid, Reginleif, Svipul, Sangrid, Hjortrimul, Gunn, Ladgerd, Sigrdrifa, and Brynhild.

It is said that whenever a child is born, the Valkyries come to bless it. They bring the goddesses of fate called Norns with them so that the Norns can set the fate of the child. Therefore, you should always put out a little gift for the Norns and the Valkyries when a child has been born. Then, as the child grows up, a Valkyrie is assigned to always be there to protect it. Wise old women say that they can see the Valkyrie standing behind you.

Some Valkyries also lived in the mounds scattered in the Scandinavian countryside. It is said that you can see them when you pass a burial mound in the evening. They dance around it as white shadows, much like the mist that hangs over the fields. But it is also said that you should be careful because you never know if they will decide to take you with them into the mound. One should be very careful with these Valkyries that wander without any living humans to attach themselves to. At night, they can come into your house and ride on your chest in your sleep. This is precisely what happened once to a man named Vanlandi.

Vanlandi was a Viking, traveling with his brother Thidrandi from Finland to Sweden. On the island of Aland, they met an old woman sitting on a mound close to the shore. She asked them to come over to her and said that she would tell them their fortune. Vanlandi felt suspicious of the old woman. He said that he was not interested in hearing old wives' tales. The old woman said that he would be better off knowing what she had to tell him. Then Thidrandi said that *he* would like to hear what she had to say to him, and he went ashore and talked with the old woman for a long time.

"What did she say?" Vanlandi asked when his brother came back.

"She told me that I will go to Iceland and build a big farm there," Thidrandi replied. "To prove that she told the truth, she said that I've lost my golden image of Frey."

Vanlandi knew that his brother always carried the image of Frey in his bag, so he demanded that Thidrandi check it. And to the surprise of both of them, the golden image of Frey was gone.

Now Vanlandi said to the woman that he would like to hear his fortune after all, but she said, "An unwise man thinks he knows it all, but he doesn't know what he ought to know: that he is not free of flaws. The lame can ride a horse; the handless can drive a herd; the deaf can win a fight; you are better off blind than burned. I am Huld and I curse you, Vanlandi!" Then she turned to Thidrandi and said, "Hail you, Thidrandi! Now you have heard the words of the High One! They're useful to the sons of men, not so useful to the sons of Jotnar. Good luck to whomever knows them. Good luck to whomever learns them. Good luck to whomever listens to them!" And upon that, she disappeared.

Vanlandi didn't know how seriously to take the stranger's curse. He tried not to think about it as he and his brother continued their travels across the sea to Sweden. Once they landed, they came to a farm that was owned by a man named Jokul and were given lodging for the night. Before they went to bed, Jokul said that if they heard a knocking on the door in the middle of the night, they should not open the door no matter what. In the middle of the night, just as they had been warned, they heard a loud knocking on the door. The visitor kept banging and banging and banging. Finally, Thidrandi became so annoyed with the knocking that he went to the door and opened it, even though he knew he was not supposed to.

It was completely dark outside, and, at first, Thidrandi couldn't see anything. Then, slowly, he realized that the darkness wasn't the night sky but a huge black cat, larger than the house, that stood in front of him with closed eyes. The cat opened its eyes and said, "Why are you still here, Thidrandi?" Then it disappeared. As soon as it disappeared, everyone heard Vanlandi screaming in his bed. He insisted that a mare was riding his chest and stomping on him, and then, all too suddenly, he died.

Thidrandi realized that Huld's curse had sent a nightmare to Vanlandi as punishment for his arrogance. As soon as he could, Thidrandi left for Iceland, following Huld's prophecy. When he came within sight of

Iceland, he took off the dragon heads on the prow of his ship so that he would not scare the spirits of the land. Then he threw overboard his god-pillar, which is a wooden pole with symbolic meaning. Once the god-pillar drifted ashore, Thidrandi sailed toward where it had landed and claimed all the land in that inlet between two cliffs, which was called a fjord. He began building his farm there.

When Thidrandi was digging a hole to place his god-pillar in, he saw a piece of gold glimmering in the sunlight. He reached down into the hole and picked it up, and just like Huld had told him, it was the golden image of Frey that he had lost on Aland. When he looked up, he saw a small black cat sitting on a rock not far from him, and that is when he understood that Huld had become his Valkyrie, the spirit that would always watch over him.

One evening some time later, Thidrandi was sitting outside, watching his sheep, when he saw nine Valkyries ride on their horses toward a large mound on his land. He became curious and followed the Valkyries to the mound, but when he climbed on top of it, they were nowhere to be seen. Then he looked down and saw that there was a hole in the mound with light shining out of it. He peeked into the hole, and there he saw the Valkyries. They were weaving on a loom, but it was no ordinary loom. The loom was made of weapons, and the Valkyries were weaving together parts of the human body, dripping with blood.

While they were weaving, they were singing the Valkyries' song, and it sounded something like this: "Let the spools on the spear-loom run! We will go where the war is, and our friends fight with weapons. Let the spools on the spear-loom run! We will go where blood drips from warriors' shields. Let the spools on the spear-loom run! Where flags fly and weapons bite, Valkyries will choose warriors for Valhall! There will be blood-red skies where the mighty maidens of war sing their song."

When they were all done weaving, the Valkyries got back on their horses and rode away toward the north. Thidrandi went home and told everyone what he had seen. The next day, the Valkyries staged a mighty battle between the Nordic kings at a place called Stiklestad. Thidrandi knew of this battle before it even began, because he had heard the Valkyries' song.

SIGRDRIFA,
THE MIGHTY VALKYRIE

I n Jotunheim, there was a great warrior named Angantyr who possessed a sword called Tyrfing. It was said to be the best sword any warrior had ever had. When Angantyr drew Tyrfing, the blade would shine bright like the sun, even if it was drawn in the dark of the night. Tyrfing was such a powerful sword that it could fight enemies all on its own and did not need a hand to be wielded. However, whenever Tyrfing was drawn out of its sheath, it could not be put back again without blood on it.

As a mighty warrior, Angantyr became a famous Viking and won much land in Midgard, the land of humans. He came to rule the place called Rauma, which lies around the Gota River in Sweden.

One day, the elf king of Alfheim came to Angantyr and asked him if he would help rescue his daughter Alfhild, who had been kidnapped by a berserk—one of Odin's bear-warriors—named Starkad. Angantyr agreed and swiftly defeated Starkad in a duel. As a result, Angantyr married Alfhild, and together they had many children. The youngest one was called Sigrdrifa, and she was the fiercest and most beautiful of the children.

When Sigrdrifa had grown into a young woman, Adils, prince of the kingdom Svealand, came to Angantyr and asked for Sigrdrifa's hand in marriage. Much time had passed since his days as a warrior, and Angantyr was now old and frail. He instructed Adils to speak to Sigrdrifa directly about his intentions. When Adils approached Sigrdrifa about his desire to marry her, she said that she would not marry a man who was weaker than herself, so he would have to prove his strength by lifting her off the ground. Adils agreed and went up to Sigrdrifa and clasped her around her waist and pulled, but nothing happened. Sigrdrifa's feet stood firmly on the ground. She did not move an inch.

Greatly disappointed that he did not earn Sigrdrifa's hand in marriage, Adils rode back home to his father's kingdom in Svealand. He sat there in the hall at his castle Upsala, brooding over what had happened at Rauma, and soon his disappointment turned to anger and scorn. Enraged that he had been bested by a woman, he gathered all his warriors and set out to go to war with Angantyr.

No one in Rauma expected this, so they were greatly surprised and not at all prepared when Adils sailed up the Gota Rriver with his army. Adils immediately burned down Angantyr's great hall at Rauma. Those who were not killed in the great hall fled to all corners of the world. Angantyr and Alfhild took three ships with them as they fled, with Alfhild and Sigrdrifa on one ship and Angantyr and the rest of the family on another.

Adils saw the three ships leaving in three different directions, and he wanted to follow the one with Sigrdrifa on it. When he saw that there was a young woman on the ship that was headed south, he believed that this was Sigrdrifa, and so he followed.

Adils pursued the ship all the way to the island called Samso. But when he finally arrived there, he discovered that it was not Sigrdrifa who was on the ship at all! Adils had followed the ship with Sigrdrifa's father, brothers, and sisters. He had mistaken one of the sisters for the woman he wanted. He attacked Angantyr and a fierce battle broke out.

Angantyr wielded Tyrfing during the battle, fearless and strong, but when Adils realized that Tyrfing was a magic sword, he used Odin's war magic and sang a *galdr* song: "I know a song, if I need it, to keep my enemies in check. I blunt their blades and their weapons won't bite!" At that, Tyrfing was rendered harmless to Adils, and Angantyr did not stand a chance in the fight. When the bloody battle was over, Adils killed everyone who had been on Angantyr's ship and buried them all in a great mound on Samso, which is called Onshog.

As the battle raged and the rest of their family was killed, Alfhild and Sigrdrifa escaped north to Norway and were shielded there by King Sigrlam of Bjarmaland. When news of the death of Angantyr and her entire family—except her mother—reached Sigrdrifa, she swore revenge. She put on armor and took a ship, the biggest ship that had ever been built. She sailed to Samso and went up to the mound called Onshog. There she spoke a verse of death *galdr* to awaken Angantyr. She said, "Angantyr, your daughter awakens you! Give me the gift of the mighty sword Tyrfing, made in ancient times by the skilled dwarfs."

Then Angantyr arose from the grave, covered in dirt, with ice and blood in his hair. He said, "Mighty maiden, Sigrdrifa! My brave daughter! None is as brave as you, who dares take the bloody sword Tyrfing from a ghoul's hand. Go now! Go to war and win much fame for our family."

At that, Sigrdrifa took Tyrfing, collected a great army of Danes and Norwegians, and then she returned to her ship and sailed toward Svealand. Adils saw the hundreds of ships as they approached, and he asked, "Who are these Spear-Danes—Geats and Goths and Gar-Dani on my shores? What kind of men are you to come here, rigged out for battle in armor and ships of war? And who is their leader—this warrior that stands in their midst, a head taller than them all, and sports such a menacing grin?" Not much was said after that, for Sigrdrifa and her army stormed Adils's palace and set everything ablaze. Sigrdrifa went straight for Adils, chopped off his head, and laid waste to his lands. It is said that his skull was used as a drinking cup at the war feast that took place after the victory.

After Sigrdrifa had had her revenge, she turned her army back over land. They marched through the woods toward her father's old kingdom in Rauma.

Unbeknownst to Sigrdrifa, Adils's son Atli had escaped with his life and hid in the mountains west of Svealand while he sent out his spies to follow Sigrdrifa. As the victorious army was on its way home in the deep woods, one of Atli's scouts spotted them. Sigrdrifa was wearing golden armor and a white dress that billowed around her like clouds. The light shining off her was so strong that it seemed like the sun itself. Her golden hair was so long that it almost reached the ground.

The scout took an arrow, broke off a thorn from a hawthorn to use for the arrow's head, and then shot the arrow straight at Sigrdrifa. The arrow pierced her golden armor and hit her right in the heart, knocking her down dead on the ground.

All her warriors stopped their marching, stricken with grief, and held a great funeral ceremony for her. They took her body and placed it on a funeral pyre on top of the mountain called Hindarfjall. They lit the fire, but the wood underneath her would not burn. Instead, the fire made a ring around her, and her body was untouched.

At that, Odin appeared before them all and declared that he had adopted Sigrdrifa as one of his Valkyries and that she would not die. She would be left asleep in the ring of fire until a warrior great and powerful enough to match her strength would one day come and wake her from her slumber.

SIGURD,
THE DRAGON SLAYER

When Adils's son Atli had defeated Sigrdrifa, he took back power in the castle Upsala and ruled Sweden much in the same way as Adils had: cruelly and selfishly. Sigvard, the king of the nearby island Adils, knew that Atli wasn't to be trusted. He wanted to create an alliance between them, so he invited Atli to join him at Jul, the midwinter feast.

The celebrations went well. There was plenty of food and drink for everyone there, and Sigvard was pleased to see that Atli was happy and enjoying himself. But then an old man wearing a dark blue cloak with a hood that covered his face came into the hall. There was complete silence in the hall as everyone stopped their celebrating to look toward the stranger. In the middle of the hall stood a mighty evergreen tree, called Barnstok, that was growing through the roof. The old man walked up to Barnstok, pulled out a sword, and thrust it into the tree so hard that it went down all the way to the hilt. The old man said, "Whoever can pull this sword from the tree will rule all Sweden!" In a flash, he was gone.

Many people tried to pull the sword out, including both Sigvard and Atli and several of their warriors, but it did not budge one bit. Thinking that removing the sword from the tree was impossible and not knowing who the old man was, everyone went back to feasting. When the guests were cheerful again, Atli said in jest, "Sigvard! Why don't you have your baby son, Sigurd, try to pull the sword out?"

Sigurd was under a year old and sleeping in his crib. It is said that the day he was born, the Norns tied golden strings under the moon and stretched them out over all the land that Sigurd would one day rule. Sigvard thought that it would be a funny joke to let baby Sigurd have a go at pulling out the sword, so he lifted the child up and placed his hand on the hilt of the sword. To everyone's astonishment, the sword came loose, and the child held it in his hand.

First, Atli was surprised, but then he grew worried about the Norns' prophecies, so he asked Sigvard if he could buy the sword. They tried to take the sword from the child's hand, but as soon as Sigurd let go of it, it fell to the ground, heavy as a rock, impossible to lift again. Furious that he could not possess the sword, Atli announced that the evening was over.

Late that night, Sigvard woke up to the sound of someone screaming, "Fire!" He rushed out of bed, and so did all his warriors. Flames were licking the walls of the hall! Sigvard and his men ran out to get some water. As soon as they came out of the hall, they were met by a flurry of arrows from Atli and his warriors.

Fortunately, Sigvard's servant Regin had foreseen Atli's betrayal, so he managed to escape with the young Sigurd out of the back of the hall. He ran with the child to the sea, where he took a boat and sailed across the ocean. In a far-off land, Regin, who knew magic, turned himself and Sigurd into wolves, and they lived in the woods, far away from people.

When Sigurd had grown into a young man, Regin told him the story of Atli's betrayal and said, "I will help you get your kingdom back. But first, you must help me. You see, before the day that the gods bound Loki, the trickster was hiding at my father Hreidmar's farm. Because of Loki's presence there, things went really bad for my father, and my brother Fafnir killed him and took all his gold. Now, Fafnir has taken the form of a giant dragon and lies at Gnithaheid on top of the pile of gold. Help me avenge my father, and you can have his gold as well as your sword."

Regin and Sigurd journeyed to Gotland, the land of Sigurd's birth, and found the sword. To that day, Sigurd was the only one who could lift it. Then they went to Gnithaheid where Fafnir the dragon lay in wait. Regin suggested that Sigurd dig a ditch and hide in it, and then when Fafnir came slithering over the ground, Sigurd could pierce his belly with the sword. Sigurd began to dig a ditch. Then, an old man wearing a dark blue cloak came by and said, "If you plan to kill Fafnir, you should dig more than one ditch. Otherwise the dragon's blood will drown you." Sigurd did as the old man had said and dug a second ditch. Then he waited for the dragon to awaken. When Fafnir finally came slithering over the ditch where Sigurd was waiting, Sigurd took his sword and stabbed Fafnir in the gut. The blood spilled out exactly the way the old man had said it would, and Sigurd was safe as the dragon lay dying.

When Fafnir was dead, Regin came out from his hiding place. He told Sigurd to cut out the dragon's heart and roast it over a fire. Regin laid down to nap as Sigurd cut out the dragon's great heart. Sigurd then sat under an oak tree, pierced the heart with his sword, and began roasting it over the fire. In the tree's branches, there sat two ravens, croaking at each other.

After some time, Sigurd took the dragon's heart out of the fire and poked at it with his thumb to see if it was done. He burned the tip of his thumb on the hot heart and quickly stuck it in his mouth to cool it. When the blood from the dragon's heart touched his lips, he could suddenly understand the speech of the ravens above him in the oak tree's branches. He heard one raven say to the other, "Look at young Sigurd, the fool! He doesn't know that Regin, the coward, is planning to eat the heart himself and use the strength from Fafnir to kill Sigurd so that he can run off with the gold."

When Sigurd heard this, he crept over to Regin and killed him in his sleep. He then took the collection of gold, which included a ring called Andvarinaut, and rode away from Gnithaheid.

As Sigurd was riding through the woods, he came by a mountain with a fire burning on its top. This was Hindarfjall, where the Valkyrie Sigrdrifa was lying in her sleep. Odin had said that she would lie here, with the arrow that had killed her still piercing her heart, until a warrior who matched her in strength came to wake her.

Sigurd rode his horse through the flames, to the beautiful Valkyrie lying on the pyre. He walked up to her, grabbed the arrow stuck in her heart, and pulled it out. Then he lifted her off the pyre and brought her out of the ring of fire. As soon as Sigrdrifa woke up and locked eyes with Sigurd, they fell in love. Here at last was the man with strength to match her own! Sigurd gave her the ring Andvarinaut as a promise that he would return as soon as he had avenged his father's death.

Leaving Sigrdrifa behind, Sigurd rode off to Svealand, where he found Atli—the prince who had killed Sigurd's father and whose servant had shot Sigrdrifa. Sigurd challenged Atli to a duel. They met and fought for days. During the battle, Sigurd chopped off Atli's leg with his mighty sword, but Atli simply fell back and rested his leg on a tree stump. Sigurd said, "You're done, and I won't fight a wounded man."

But Atli said, "I should be able to hold out if I can just get a drink of water. Will you give me that?"

Sigurd said, "As long as you don't trick me."

And Atli replied, "I won't trick you."

Sigurd went to a brook and got water for Atli, but when he bent over to give him the water, Atli struck Sigurd's head and gave him a deep wound. Sigurd said, "You're a coward! I trusted you, but you betrayed me!"

It was true. Atli was greedy and wanted all of Sweden to himself, and he would lie and cheat in order to get it. The fighting continued but, in the end, Sigurd was the mightier warrior and killed Atli. He rode back to Sigrdrifa, but the wound on his head was too deep, and he died in her arms when they were rejoined. Sigrdfria had been brought back to life by the one man who matched her in strength, but now he was no longer. It is said that Sigrdrifa died again that day, this time of grief.

RAGNAROK,
THE END OF THE WORLD

ome say that when Sigurd and Sigrdrifa died, they were reborn. Others say that they went to Niflheim, the world of the dead, but could come back when people called on them and used *galdr* magic. Many people said that they saw Sigurd and Sigrdrifa after their death.

One such person was a man named Gagnrad, who traveled far and wide. When he was walking through the high mountains, he came upon a cave, and, hearing voices from inside, he thought, *When you find yourself wandering astray, company is always a delight.*

He went inside to greet the people he heard, but the cave was dark, and he couldn't see anybody. He called out and asked if there was anyone in there, and then he saw Sigrdrifa, as beautiful as the day she died. She emerged from the darkness in the back of the cave and asked, "Why do you awaken me?"

Gagnrad stammered, "I- I thought I heard voices in here."

Sigrdrifa said, "All you heard was the whispering of the world. It is in the wind. It is in the trees; it is in their leaves. It is in the grass and rocks and the babbling brooks of water running down the mountains."

Gagnrad said, "Forgive me for disturbing you. I will go now," and he turned around to leave.

But behind him, all Gagnrad saw was darkness. Then he heard Sigrdrifa's voice again, "I will tell you spells from ancient times. What I saw and what I remember. Further, I see into the future. I see the darkness of the gods of victory." Gagnrad turned around to face Sigrdrifa, but there was no light by which to see her. Then she began her prophecy. This is what she told Gagnrad:

"Listen to me, all holy beings, higher and lower, descendants of Heimdall! I have seen a prisoner deep in the earth. It is Loki, plotting harm on us all. His wife Sigyn sits by him, watching over her husband, but she feels no joy. A river runs from the east. Its water is made of swords, and it is called Slith. A hall, its roof is made of serpents, stands farthest from the sun on the northern beaches of Nastrond. People walk the road to Hel and wade through heavy streams.

"I see those who swear false, murderers and thieves, all torn apart by the hungry wolf Fenrir. He is filled with the blood of the doomed. He reddens the sky with the blood of the gods. The sun turns black and the weather turns nasty. The winter lasts for three seasons.

"A herdsman sits on a grave mound. In the gallows above him crows a bright red rooster. In the halls of Valhall crows a golden rooster, which awakens Odin's warriors. In the halls of Hel, a soot-red rooster crows for the Draugar—the undead. The wolf howls before a deep cave. Soon his bonds will break, and he will run ravenous across the sky. Brothers will fight and kill one another; bonds of kinship will be broken. Times are hard: axe-age, sword-age, shields are split; wind-age, wolf-age, before the world falls. None shall spare each other.

"The watchman Heimdall blows his horn; Odin speaks with Mimir's head. Jotunheim groans, and the gods meet at their assembly. The dwarfs howl before their stone doors. The mighty, ancient ash tree Yggdrasill trembles. Loki breaks free and the Jotun Surt follows him. Surt's fire swallows the road to Hel. Jormungand the sea serpent writhes and wiggles in the sea; the waves swallow the land. The eagle with an ash-pale beak shrieks, and the ship of nails brings the Draugar back from the dead. The ship sails from the east with Loki at the helm and Surt at the port, and all Muspell's warriors will follow. Surt's sword shines brighter than the sun. Mountains crumble, trolls rumble, warriors wade to Hel, and the sky is torn apart. The sun is black, the land is sinking, the bright stars fall from heaven. Flames swallow the world tree. Fire flies to heaven itself."

As Sigrdrifa was speaking, images of destruction appeared before Gagnrad on the wall of the cave. He saw the gruesome end of the world, just as Sigrdrifa spoke it. In the visions he saw, the god Frey fought Surt in a fierce battle that brought them both to their knees. Thor met Jormungand and struck down the serpent, but he could only take nine steps away from it before he collapsed from its poison. Odin rode Sleipnir towards Fenrir, but the war god was swallowed whole by the mighty wolf. Flames and smoke rose from all corners of the world. The gods died one by one, and Asgard turned to dust. Yggdrasill was ablaze, and its trunk turned from bright white to dark soot. Soon, the tree cracked and fell over the world. Nothing was left standing.

But then Gagnrad saw Vidar, Odin's warrior son, fight Fenrir the wolf with his sword. He placed his foot on Fenrir's bottom jaw and held the upper jaw with his hand. Then he stuck the sword deep in the wolf's mouth and pierced its heart.

These images faded. It was pitch black in the cave, and Gagnrad was terrified. He called out, "Sigrdrifa! I have seen the demise of the gods.

I have seen Ragnarok! Tell me one last thing: Will there be a world after this one?"

Sigrdrifa said, "I see ahead, even further into the future. Earth rises from the sea, evergreen and lush. Waterfalls rush from the mountains and a new sun shines brighter than before. Plants grow and blossoms bloom; bees and birds play in the meadows. Eagles fly high above, and fish frolic in the streams. Unsown fields grow plentiful. The two brothers, Balder and Hother, will meet on the eternal plains, find the ancient runes, and build new halls. People will live cheerfully in a new grove, and the world will be at peace. All harm will be healed. I have said enough. Now I must sink down to the depths from where I came."

And that is how the story of Ragnarok, the end of the world, concludes.

The Norse Families

otnar were the first beings on earth. They were related to ice and fire. The Jotnar were neither good nor bad. They were the natural forces in the world, and sometimes the gods had to fight them to make the world pleasant for humans. The very first Jotun was named Ymir, and he created many of the other Jotnar with his hands and feet.

One of the Jotnar was named Bolthorn, and he had a daughter called Bestla.

Bestla had the sons Odin, Vili, and Ve with Burr. Burr rose from the rocks of the earth.

Odin was the ruler of the gods and the god of war, magic, wisdom, and poetry. He had Balder, Hother, and Hermoder with Frigg, the daughter of Fjorgyn. No one knows where Fjorgyn came from, but Frigg was the mother goddess of the marshes.

Balder was a warrior god, and he was married to Nanna, the goddess of the household. They had the son Forseti, who was the god of justice.

With Rind, Odin had Bui, and with Grid, he had Vidar. Both Vidar and Bui were warrior gods in charge of revenge and renewal.

With Jord, Odin also had Thor, the god of humans. Thor had a daughter named Thrud with the goddess Sif, who also had the son Ull. Thrud was a goddess of strength, and Ull was a god of the woods, skiing, and mountains. With Jarnsaxa, Thor also had the sons Magni and Modi. They were gods for strength and resilience.

Njord was the god of ships and seafaring. He was the father of Frey and Freya. Freya was a goddess of war and love, and she was married to Od, the traveling god. Together, they had the daughters Hnoss and Gersimi, who was a warden of beauty. Frey was married to Gerd, but they did not have any children. Frey was the god of kings, and Gerd was the goddess of fertile fields.

Skadi was the daughter of Thjazi, a Jotun and eagle god. Skadi was the goddess of the mountains, wolves, hunting, and skiing. Njord was married to Skadi, and their daughter was Ran, who was married to Agir, the god of the sea. Ran was the goddess of drowned seafarers, and with Agir she had nine daughters: Himingleva, Dufa, Blodughadda, Hefring, Unn, Hronn, Bylgia, Bara, and Kolga.

Loki was the son of the Jotun Farbauti and the goddess Laufey. He was married to Sigyn, and they had the sons Nari and Narfi.

Together with Angerboda, Loki also had the son Fenrir. Loki was also the mother of Odin's horse Sleipnir, whom he got with the horse Svadilfari.

Tyr was the son of the Jotun Hymir. Tyr was a god of bravery and battle, but Hymir was a grim frost-Jotun. Heimdall had nine unnamed mothers. He was the watchman of the gods, and he guarded the entrance to Asgard.

Idun was the goddess of youth and renewal, the eternal return. She was married to Bragi, the god of poets. There were also the gods Sol and Mani, sun and moon. They were sister and brother, and they were the children of Mundilfari and Nott.

GLOSSARY

Adils (E-deels): A legendary king

Agir (A-geer): God of the sea

Aland (O-land): An island

Alfheim (Elf-hame): The land of the elves; Frey's abode

Alfhild (Elf-heeld): A legendary princess

Alfrik (Elf-reeck): A dwarf

Am (Ahm): A demon

Amsvartnir (Ahm-swart-neer): A lake

Andvari (And-vah-ree): A dwarf

Andvarinaut (And-vah-ree-nawt): A ring

Angantyr (Angan-teer): A legendary hero

Angerboda (Anger-boa-tha): A troll

Asgard (Ahs-gard): The world of the gods

Ask (Ah-sk): The first man

Atli (Ah-tlee): A legendary king

Audhumbla (Uh-th-humbla): The primordial cow

Aurvandil (Uhr-van-deel): A hero

Balder (Ball-dur): A god; Odin's son

Bara (Bah-ra): A goddess; Ran's daughter

Barnstok (Barn-stock): A sacred tree

Barri (Bah-ree): A sacred grove

Baugi (Buh-gee): A demon

Bele (Beh-leh): A demon

Berling (Bear-ling): A dwarf

berserk (bear-sark): Odin's bear-warrior; singular

berserkir (bear-sar-keer): Odin's bear-warriors; plural

Bestla (Bayst-lah): A demon; mother of Odin, Vili, and Ve

Bjarmaland (By-ahrma-land): The northern lands in Scandinavia

Blodughadda (Bloth-uh-heddah): A goddess; Ran's daughter

Bolthorn (Ball-thorn): A demon; father of Bestla

Bolverk (Ball-vark): A name for Odin

Bragi (Brag-ee): God of poetry

Brising's necklace (Bree-seeng's necklace): Freya's necklace

Brokk (Brack): A dwarf

Brynhild (Breen-held): A Valkyrie

Bui (Boo-ee): A god; Odin's son

Bylgia (Beel-gya): A goddess; Ran's daughter

Disir (Dee-seer): The goddesses; collective

Draugar (Druh-gahr): The undead; ghosts

Draupnir (Drup-neer): Odin's magical ring

Dromi (Druh-mee): A chain

Dufa (Doo-fah): A goddess; Ran's daughter

Dvalinn (Duh-ah-leen): A dwarf

Eikthyrnir (Ayck-thur-neer): A legendary deer

Eir (Air): Goddess of healing

Eitri (Ay-tree): A dwarf

Embla (Ahm-blah): The first woman

Fafnir (Fahf-neer): A legendary man and dragon

Farbauti (Fahrbuhtee): A Jotun; Loki's father

Fenja (Fahn-yah): A troll-woman

Fenrir (Fahn-reer): A demon wolf

Fensalir (Fahn-sah-leer): Frigg's abode

Finnmark (Feen-mark): The northern parts of Scandinavia

Fjalar (Fyah-lar): A dwarf

Fjorgyn (Fyurh-geen): Frigg's father

Folkvangar (Folk-vahng-ar): Freya's lands

Forseti (For-sah-tee): God of justice

Frey (Fray): God of kings and fertility

Freya (Fray-ah): Goddess of love and warfare

Frigg (Frick): Goddess of motherhood

frua (froo-ah): The word for "lady"

Fulla (Fool-ah): A goddess; Frigg's servant

Gagnrad (Gawn-roth): A legendary man

Galar (Gah-lah): A dwarf

galdr (gahl-dur): The word for "song-magic"

gandr (gahn-dur): The word for "staff-magic"

Ganglot (Gahng-lot): Hel's servant

Gefiun (Gaf-yuhn): A goddess

Gefn (Gafn): A goddess; a name for Freya

Geirondul (Gay-ruhn-dool): A Valkyrie

Geirrod (Gay-roth): A demon

Gerd (Gairth): Goddess of the fields

Gersimi (Gair-see-mee): A goddess; daughter of Freya

Ginnungagap (Geen-uhn-gah-gap): The primordial void

Gjalp (Gyalp): A demon

Gjoll (Gyoh-tl): A river

Gleipnir (Glayp-neer): A chain

Gna (Gnaw): A goddess; Frigg's servant

Gnithaheid (Gnee-tha-hayth): A legendary plain

Goll (Guh-tl): A Valkyrie

Gota (Yoh-ta): A river in Sweden

Gotland (Got-land): An island

Greip (Grayp): A demon

Grer (Grayr): A demon

Grjotun (Gryoh-tun): A place in Jotunheim

Groa (Grow-a): A Jotun woman

Grotti (Groh-tee): A millstone

Gullfaxi (Gooh-tl-faxee): A horse

Gullveig (Gooh-tl-vayg): A goddess

Gungnir (Goong-neer): Odin's spear

Gunlod (Goon-luh-th): A Jotun woman

Gunn (Goohn): A Valkyrie

Gylfi (Geel-fee): A legendary king

Gymir (Gee-meer): A legendary king

Gymisgard (Gee-mees-gahr-th): Agir's abode

Hanginkjapta (Hang-een-kyap-ta): A demon

Hefring (Hap-ring): A goddess; daughter of Ran

Heid (Hayth): A goddess

Heimdall (Hame-dahl): The watchman of the gods

Hel (Hel): Goddess of the dead

Helgafell (Hel-gah-feh-tl): A holy mountain

Herfjotur (Har-fyuh-toor): A Valkyrie

Hermoder (Har-moth-urh): A god; son of Odin

Hild (Heeld): A Valkyrie

Himinbjorg (Hee-meen-byorg): Heimdall's abode

Himingleva (Hee-meen-glay-vah): A goddess; daughter of Ran

Hindarfjall (Heen-dar-fya-tl): A holy mountain

Hjadningavik (Hyath-neenga-veek): A place

Hjortrimul (Hyurt-ree-muhl): A Valkyrie

Hlidskjalf (Hleeth-skyalf): Odin's throne

Hlin (Hleen): A Valkyrie

Hlokk (Hlock): A Valkyrie

Hnitbjorg (Hneet-byorg): A mountain

Hnoss (Hnuss): A goddess; Freya's daughter

Honir (Huh-neer): A god

Horn (Hurn): A name for Freya

Hother (Ho-thurh): A god; Odin's son

Hreid's Sea (Hrayth's Sea): A sea

Hreidmar (Hrayth-mahr): A sorcerer

Hrimnir (Hreem-neer): A Jotun

Hrist (Hreest): A Valkyrie

Hronn (Hruhn): A goddess; daughter of Ran

Hrungnir (Hroong-neer): A Jotun

Huginn (Hoo-ween): Odin's raven

Huld (Hoold): A volva; sorceress

Huldra (Hool-drah): A supernatural being; singular

Huldur (Hool-door): A supernatural being; plural

Hymir (Hee-meer): A Jotun

Hyrrokkin (Heer-ruhk-een): A Jotun; a demon

Idavoll (Eetha-vuhl): The eternal plains

Idun (Eeth-oon): A goddess

Ivaldi (Ee-vahl-dee): A dwarf

Jarnsaxa (Yarn-saxa): A Jotun woman

Jarnvid (Yarn-veeth): A forest

Jokul (Yo-kuhl): A king

Jord (Yurd): Goddess of the earth

Jormungand (Yurh-moon-gand): The serpent of the sea

Jotnar (Yuht-nar): Supernatural beings; plural

Jotun (Yuh-toon): Supernatural being; singular

Jotunheim (Yuh-toon-hame): Home of the Jotnar

Jul (Yool): The Viking New Year

Kolga (Kuhl-gah): A goddess; daughter of Ran

Kvasir (Qua-seer): A legendary figure

Ladgerd (Lath-gurhd): A Valkyrie

Laufey (Luw-fay): A goddess; Loki's mother

Leyding (Lay-theeng): A chain

Lofn (Lufn): Goddess of promises

Loki (Luh-kee): The trickster god

Lopt (Luhpt): Another name for Loki

Magni (Mahng-nee): A god; son of Thor

Malar (Mehlahr): A lake in Sweden

Mardol (Mahr-duhl): A name for Freya

Megingjord (May-ing-gyurth): Thor's belt

Menja (Man-ya): A troll-woman

Midgard (Meeth-gahrth): Middle Earth; home of humans

midgards verjandi (meeth-gahrths varh-yan-dee): A name for Thor

Mimir (Mee-meer): A god; Odin's talking head

Mist (Meest): A Valkyrie

Mjollnir (Myuhl-neer): Thor's hammer

Modgud (Muth-gooth): Warden of the entrance to the underworld

Modi (Mothi): A god; son of Thor

Mokkurkalfi (Moh-koor-kawl-fee): A troll

Mundilfari (Moon-deel-fah-ree): A god

Muninn (Moon-een): Odin's raven

Muspell (Moos-patl): The realm of fire

Muspellheim (Moo-spa-tl-hame): The fire in the underworld

Nagrind (Naw-greend): The gate to the world of the dead

Narfi (Nahr-vee): Loki's son

Nari (Nahr-ee): Loki's son

Nastrond (Naw-strund): The northern beaches

Nidavellir (Nee-tha-vall-eer): The world of the dwarfs

Nidhogg (Neeth-hoog): The serpent in the underworld

Niflheim (Nee-fuhl-hame): The world of the dead

Njord (Nyurth): The god of ships and sailing

Noatun (Nuh-ah-toon): Njord's abode

Norn (Norn): Goddess of fate

Nott (Noht): A goddess

Od (Oath): Freya's husband

Odin (Oath-een): God of war, wisdom, the runes

Odrerir (Uth-ray-reer): The pot that contains the mead of poetry

Ondurdis (Uhn-door-dees): A name for Skadi

Onshog (Uhns-hoog): A mound

Radgrid (Rath-greeth): A Valkyrie

Ragnarok (Rack-nah-ruck): The end of the world

Ran (Rawn): Goddess of the sea

Randgrid (Rand-greeth): A Valkyrie

Rauma (Ruh-mah): A kingdom in Sweden

Regin (Ray-een): A legendary man

Reginleif (Ray-een-layf): A Valkyrie

Roskva (Ruhs-qua): Human servant of Thor

sæl (sah-il): The word for "hello"

Saga (Saw-gah): Goddess of history

Samso (Sam-suh): An island

Sangrid (San-greeth): A Valkyrie

seidr (sayth-uhr): Magic

Sessrumnir (Sass-room-neer): Freya's abode

Sif (Seef): A goddess; Thor's wife

Sigrdrifa (See-guhr-dree-fah): A Valkyrie

Sigrlam (See-guhr-lahm): A legendary king

Sigurd (See-goor-th): A legendary hero

Sigvard (Seeg-varth): A legendary king

Sigyn (See-geen): A goddess; Loki's wife

Siofn (See-uhfn): Goddess of love

Skadi (Skah-thee): Goddess of the mountains

skald (skawld): Viking poet

Skati's Grove (Skah-tee's Grove): A grove

Skegold (Skay-guhld): A Valkyrie

Skogul (Skuh-gool): A Valkyrie

Sleipnir (Slayp-neer): Odin's horse

Slith (Sleeth): A river

Snotra (Snuht-rah): Goddess of knowledge

Starkad (Star-kath): A legendary figure

Stiklestad (Steek-lah-stath): A place of a legendary battle

Surt (Sert): A Jotun

Suttung (Soot-oong): A Jotun

Svadilfari (Svath-eel-fah-ree): A horse

Svealand (Svay-a-land): A kingdom in Sweden

Svipul (Sveep-ool): A Valkyrie

Syn (Seen): Goddess of denial

Syr (Seer): A name for Freya

Tanngniost (Tan-gnee-ust): Thor's goat

Tanngnist (Tan-gneest): Thor's goat

Thidrandi (Theeth-ran-dee): A legendary hero

Thjalfi (Thyal-fee): A god; Thor's helper

Thjazi (Thyat-see): A Jotun

Thor (Thor): God of thunder

Thorolf (Thor-olf): A legendary Viking

Thrud (Throoth): Thor's daughter

Thrudheim (Throoth-hame): Thor's abode

Thrym (Threem): A Jotun

Thrymheim (Threem-hame): A place in Jotunheim

Tyr (Teer): God of courage

Tyrfing (Teer-feeng): A legendary sword

ulfhednar (oolf-hath-nahr): Odin's wolf-warriors

Ull (Oo-tl): God of the forests

Unn (Oon): A goddess; daughter of Ran

Upsala (Oop-sah-lah): A castle in Sweden

Urd (Oorth): A Norn

Valhall (Vahl-hahl): Odin's abode

Valkyrie (Vahl-keer-yah): War goddess

Vanlandi (Vahn-lan-dee): A legendary hero

Var (Va-uhr): Goddess of oaths

Ve (Vyuh): A god; Odin's brother

Vidar (Vee-thar): A god; Odin's son

Vili (Vee-lee): A god; Odin's brother

Vimur (Vee-muhr): A river

Volund (Vuh-loond): A legendary king

volur (vuh-loor): Prophetesses; plural

volva (vuhl-vah): Prophetess; singular

Vor (Vuhr): Goddess of diligence.

Yggdrasill (Eeg-drah-see-tl): The world tree

Ymir (Ee-meer): The primordial Jotun

Zealand (Zealand): A Danish island

REFERENCES

Asbjørnsen, Peter Christen, and Jørgen Moe. *Norwegian Folktales*. Translated by Tiina Nunnally. Minneapolis: University of Minnesota Press, 2019.

Attwood, Katrina, trans. "The Saga of Gunnlaug Serpent-Tongue." In *The Sagas of Icelanders*, edited by Jane Smiley. New York: Penguin Books, 2000.

Crawford, Jackson, trans. *The Poetic Edda: Stories of the Norse Gods and Heroes*. Indianapolis: Hackett Classics, 2015.

Crawford, Jackson, trans. *The Saga of the Volsungs with The Saga of Ragnar Lothbrok*. Indianapolis: Hackett Classics, 2017.

Fisher, Peter, trans., and Hilda R. E. Davidson, ed. *Saxo Grammaticus: The History of the Danes, Books 1-9*. Rochester: Boydell and Brewers, 2008.

Gúðrúnarson, Eilíf. "Þorsdrápa." In *Edda*, translated and edited by Anthony Faulkes. London: Everyman, 2005.

Helm, Karl, Wilhelm Braune, and Ernst Ebbinghaus. "The Second Merseburg Charm." In *Althochdeutsches Lesebuch: Zusammengestellt und mit Wörterbuch versehen*. Tübingen, Germany: De Gruyter, 2005.

Hollander, Lee M., trans. "The Saga of the Ynglings." In *Heimskringla: History of the Kings of Norway*. Austin: University of Texas Press, 1991.

Lindow, John. *Norse Mythology: A Guide to the Gods, Heroes, Rituals, and Beliefs*. Oxford: Oxford University Press, 2001.

Lönnrot, Elias. *The Kalevala.* Translated by Keith Bosley. Oxford: Oxford World's Classics, 2009.

McKinnell, John, Rudolf Simek, and Klaus Düwel. *Runes, Magic and Religion: A Sourcebook.* Wien: Fassbaender, 2004.

Þióðólfr ór Hvíni. "Haustlöng." In *Edda*, translated and edited by Anthony Faulkes. London: Everyman, 2005.

Quinn, Judy, trans. "The Saga of the People of Eyri." In Vol. 4 of *The Complete Sagas of Icelanders*, edited by Vidar Hreinsson. Reykjavík: Leifur Eiriksson Publication, 1997.

Simek, Rudolf. *Dictionary of Northern Mythology.* Rochester: D. S. Brewer, 2007.

Simpson, Jacqueline, trans. *Icelandic Folktales and Legends.* Cheltenham: The History Press, 2009.

Sturluson, Snorri. *Edda.* Translated and edited by Anthony Faulkes. London: Everyman, 2005.

Turville-Petre, Gabriel, trans. *Hervarar saga ok Heiðreks.* London: Viking Society for Northern Research, 1976.

Uggason, Úlfr. "Húsdrápa." In *Edda*, translated and edited by Anthony Faulkes. London: Everyman, 2005.

Vigfússon, Guðbrandur, and Carl Rikard Unger. *Flateyjarbók.* Christiania (Oslo): P. T. Mallings Forlagboghandel, 1860.

Wawn, Andrew, trans. "The Saga of the People of Vatnsdal." In *The Sagas of Icelanders*, edited by Jane Smiley. New York: Penguin Books, 2000.

FURTHER READING

Asbjørnsen, Peter Christen, and Jørgen Moe. *Norwegian Folktales.* Translated by Tiina Nunnally. Minneapolis: University of Minnesota Press, 2019.

Crawford, Jackson, trans. *The Poetic Edda: Stories of the Norse Gods and Heroes.* Indianapolis: Hackett Classics, 2015.

Crossley-Holland, Kevin, and Jeffrey Alan Love. *Norse Myths: Tales of Odin, Thor and Loki.* Somerville: Candlewick Studio, 2017.

Kiddle. "Norse Mythology Facts for Kids." kids.kiddle.co/Norse_mythology.

Lindow, John. *Norse Mythology: A Guide to the Gods, Heroes, Rituals, and Beliefs.* Oxford: Oxford University Press, 2001.

Simpson, Jacqueline, trans. *Icelandic Folktales and Legends.* Cheltenham: The History Press, 2009.

Smiley, Jane, ed. *The Sagas of Icelanders.* New York: Penguin Books, 2001.

Sturluson, Snorri. *Edda.* Translated and edited by Anthony Faulkes. London: Everyman, 2005.

INDEX

ABOUT THE AUTHOR

 **DR. MATHIAS NORDVIG** has a PhD in Nordic mythology from Aarhus University in Denmark, his native country. He has been teaching Viking studies, Norse mythology, Scandinavian folklore, and Arctic culture at the University of Colorado at Boulder since 2015. He runs a YouTube channel called *The Nordic Mythology Channel* with the attached website NordicMythologyChannel.com. He also has a podcast with Daniel Farrand, the co-owner of the clothing company Horns of Odin, which is called *The Nordic Mythology Podcast.* In addition to publishing both research and popular fiction about Nordic mythology, Dr. Nordvig works with musicians and visual artists to create inspiring music and art about the Viking Age and Norse mythology.